BEYOND GRIT WORKBOOK

TEN POWERFUL PRACTICES TO GAIN THE HIGH-PERFORMANCE EDGE

By Cindra Kamphoff, Ph.D.

ISBN: 978-1-63489-108-0

Library of Congress Catalog Number: 2017961578
Printed in the United States of America
First Printing: 2018
22   21   20   19   18   5   4   3   2

Cover design by Nupoor Gordon
Illustration designed by Nicole Mueller
Interior design by Kim Morehead

Wise Ink Creative Publishing
807 Broadway St. NE, Suite 46
Minneapolis, MN 55413
wiseink.com

To order, visit www.BeyondGrit.com. Reseller discounts available.

To my clients and graduate students.
I am deeply grateful for you!

Contents

Introduction

I am grateful that you have chosen to use this workbook, which was written as a companion to *Beyond Grit: Ten Powerful Practices to Gain the High-Performance Edge.* It was in this book that I outlined the High Performance Mindset—a purposeful, daily pursuit of excellence—and the ten powerful practices you can use to gain a high-performance edge. These are the practices that represent the psychological profile that leads to the greatness and mastery we all want in our own lives.

This workbook was designed with you in mind. It is packed full of strategies to help you adopt and develop the High Performance Mindset, which allows you to become *mentally strong*—meaning you can take control of your thoughts, your actions, and your destiny. You can grab hold of the goals in front of you no matter how beyond your reach they may seem.

I wrote this workbook to help *you* become mentally strong. I'm psyched you have a copy! Being mentally strong is the difference between thriving in your relationships or not, being cut from your team or excelling, earning that bonus or losing your job, taking a monster risk and having it pay off or playing it safe and remaining stagnant. Your relationships, career, health, dreams, and life's purpose will not flourish if you're not mentally strong.

Every one of us has the desire to move toward excellence in our lives. But the tough part is knowing *how* to do that. The how is the secret sauce. This workbook helps you go deeper into the *"how"* presented in the original book. It provides application exercises, a way to score yourself on a self-assessment of the ten practices, a place to record your thoughts about mindset, and help in going deeper to apply the ten practices to your life.

Here are a few tips as you are working through this workbook:

- Please mark it up. Complete the exercises and write in the margins. You can get colored pens or pencils to help your ideas and thoughts stand out. Make lots of notes for yourself as you go through the exercises.

- Jump around. I'd encourage you to start with Grit, the first Practice, but from there feel free to read as you like. You could go to the Practices that you struggle with first, and then expand to others.

- You can use the workbook on your own for your personal development, or you can use it as part of an athletic team, small group of friends/coworkers, or a book club or study. It will also be more powerful if you go through the workbook on your own and reflect on each question before discussing it in a group setting as part of a team or book club.

- Before you begin each practice, I'd encourage you to go back and reread its section in *Beyond Grit* to help you go deep in its application.

- Share your experiences. Talk to a friend, family member, or teammate about what you learned going through the exercises. Tell them about your goals and the commitments you have made to yourself. Ask for their support.

- Have fun and explore your potential. You have so much inside you that you haven't even tapped. Use the exercises in the workbook to help you!

Remember, you may think that becoming mentally strong and mastering your mindset is like riding a bike—once you learn it, you can always do it—but actually living the High Performance Mindset requires ongoing, daily attention. The world's best know this is true. This workbook helps you Live and Teach the material. As you conclude each practice, you'll find a few things to record on your Grit Board.

I can't wait to hear from you on what you gained from this workbook, and see a picture of your Grit Board. Feel free to send me an email at Cindra@cindrakamphoff.com or a tweet @Mentally_Strong. Let's get gritty and be mentally strong!

Exercise: Get Ready to Make a Grit Board

To help you get gritty and develop the High Performance Mindset, develop a Grit Board. All you need to get started is an 11 x 17 poster board. Keep it handy as you read, as you'll use this board to record things for each practice in this book. When your grit board is complete, you can frame it and hang it in your home, office, or locker room. My grit board is posted right above my computer. It was in my view as I wrote this book! You can find instructions and examples of Grit Boards at beyondgrit.com/bonus.

The 10 Practices – An Overview

Beyond Grit is organized around these ten practices, techniques that represent a psychological profile leading to the greatness and mastery we all want in our own lives. These practices are supported by scientific research in sport and performance psychology, positive psychology, and neuroscience. Some of this research I conducted personally in my role as a professor; other studies I read and applied to my consulting practice.

High performers in sports, business, and life have all mastered the ten practices at the core of this book. These practices are what differentiate the world's best from the average. They get you out of your own way so you can show up as yourself, ready to move into your Courage Zone. It's beyond the grit that leads you to the High Performance Mindset, ready to think like the world's best performers.

The Top 10 Practices of the World's Best are:

1. The world's best *are gritty*. They know what they want and they know why they want it. In the face of adversity and setbacks, they go after their goals with deep commitment.

2. The world's best are *clear on their purpose*. They own why they do what they do. They keep their why front and center. This purpose keeps them motivated and hungry when the going gets tough.

3. The world's best *are a master of their thoughts*. They are intentional with their

self-talk. They exhibit powerful, positive, and possibility-oriented thinking patterns focused on process.

4. The world's best *know themselves to master themselves*. They understand themselves and their tendencies, and are in tune with their thoughts, emotions, and actions. They know they need to master themselves to be successful.

5. The world's best *dominate the controllables*. They dominate what they can control—their attitude, preparation, and effort—instead of what they cannot.

6. The world's best *own the moment*. They stay present-moment focused. They recognize that they can't control the past or the future, but they are empowered to reach their highest potential when they are engaged in the present moment.

7. The world's best *choose empowering emotions*. They thrive because they regularly experience positive emotions. They know that when people

8. The world's best *own who they are*. They make the conscious choice to show up as themselves every day and in every interaction. They know who they are and own who they are.

9. The world's best *live and let go*. They know that people are not perfect. They are kind to themselves, let go of their mistakes quickly after learning from them, and decide to live life full-out.

10. The world's best *choose their courage zone*. They feel uncomfortable regularly. When we stay in our comfort zone, we don't grow. High performers know that magic happens in their courage zone.

BEYOND GRIT WORKSHOP
PRESENTED BY DR. CINDRA KAMPHOFF

TOP 10 PRACTICES OF THE WORLD'S BEST

1 GET GRITTY

The world's best know what they want and why they want it. In face of adversity and set-backs, they go after their goals with deep commitment.

2 GET CLEAR ON YOUR PURPOSE

The world's best know why they do what they do. They keep their "why" front and center. This purpose keeps them motivated and hungry when the going gets tough.

3 MASTER YOUR THOUGHTS

The world's best are intentional with their self-talk. They exhibit powerful, positive, and possibility-oriented thoughts focused on the process.

P^4

4 KNOW YOURSELF TO MASTER YOURSELF

The world's best understand themselves, their tendencies, and are in-tune with their thoughts, emotions, and actions. They know themselves to be successful.

SUCCESS
What people think it looks like   What it really looks like

5 DOMINATE THE CONTROLLABLES

The world's best dominate what they have control over - their attitude, preparation, and effort - instead of what they cannot.

APE

6 OWN THE MOMENT

The world's best stay present moment focused. They recognize that they can't control the past or the future but they are empowered to reach their highest potential when they are engaged in the present.

NOW
Tomorrow
Yesterday

7 CHOOSE EMPOWERING EMOTIONS

The world's best thrive because they regularly experience positive emotions. They know that when people experience 3 positive emotions to every 1 negative emotion, they flourish.

3:1

8 OWN WHO YOU ARE

The world's best make the conscious choice to show up as themselves every day and in every interaction. They know who they are and own who they are.

AUTHENTICITY
100%
GUARANTEED

9 LIVE AND LET GO

The world's best know that people are not perfect. They are kind to themselves, let go of their mistakes quickly after learning from them and decide to live life full-out.

MISTAKES

10 CHOOSE YOUR COURAGE ZONE

The world's best feel uncomfortable regularly. When we stay in our comfort zone, we don't grow. High performers know that magic happens outside of the comfort zone.

YOUR COMFORT ZONE
MAGIC

To learn more about the world's best, visit
BEYONDGRIT.COM

To start working with Dr. Kamphoff, visit
CINDRAKAMPHOFF.COM

Download a PDF of this image at BeyondGrit.com/Bonus

Beyond Grit Questionnaire

The purpose of the Beyond Grit Questionnaire is to help you know where you are in practicing the 10 Practices of the World's Best. This questionnaire will give you an idea of the areas you may want to focus on throughout this workbook. To help you monitor your progress, you can retake the questionnaire after you have completed the workbook.

On the following two pages, read each statement and, using your best judgment, circle the number that best corresponds to how well you perform each practice. Remember, be honest—there are no right or wrong answers!

1. Not like me at all

2. Not much like me

3. Somewhat like me

4. Mostly like me

5. Very much like me

Beyond Grit Questionnaire

Get Gritty					
1. I have overcome setbacks to reach an important goal.	1	2	3	4	5
2. I have my long-term and short-term goals written down.	1	2	3	4	5
3. I rarely get frustrated when I experience a setback on my way to reaching my goals.	1	2	3	4	5
Get Clear on Your Purpose					
4. I know why I do what I do and remind myself of this daily.	1	2	3	4	5
5. I have considered the purpose of my life and use that purpose to guide my actions and decisions.	1	2	3	4	5
6. I know the things that I am uniquely designed to do and make decisions to engage these things often.	1	2	3	4	5
Master Your Thoughts					
7. I am great at mastering my thoughts and addressing my automatic negative thinking.	1	2	3	4	5
8. Most of my self-talk throughout my day is powerful, positive, and focused on the possibilities for my life.	1	2	3	4	5
9. I am great at viewing difficulties as exciting challenges.	1	2	3	4	5
Know Yourself to Master Yourself					
10. I understand myself and work to master my thoughts, feelings, and actions.	1	2	3	4	5

11. I regularly feel in control of my response to stressful or difficult situations.	1	2	3	4	5
12. I know what it feels like to be at my best and I consistently get there.	1	2	3	4	5

Dominate the Controllables

13. I rarely get worked up or negatively focus on things I can't control such as other people, the weather, or my opponent.	1	2	3	4	5
14. I take responsibility for my actions and decisions and am in control of my life.	1	2	3	4	5
15. I rarely believe that the worst-case scenario will happen.	1	2	3	4	5

Own the Moment

16. My mind stays focused on the present moment most of my day. I don't experience much fear, anxiety, or regret.	1.	2	3	4	5
17. When the consequences matter the most, I can stay focused in the present moment.	1	2	3	4	5
18. I have the discipline to stay focused on the process or the small things I need to do to be my best.	1	2	3	4	5

Choose Empowering Emotions

19. I generally experience more positive emotions (such as confidence, happiness, gratitude) during my day as negative emotions (such as frustration, anxiety, anger).	1	2	3	4	5
20. I have a strong belief and confidence in my ability. I believe I will be successful.	1	2	3	4	5

21. I imagine being successful in the future or the past regularly throughout my week.	1	2	3	4	5

Own Who You Are

22. I can be myself in situations at work, with my family, and in public places where I don't know anyone.	1	2	3	4	5
23. I can regularly be myself instead of trying to be someone I am not.	1	2	3	4	5
24. I rarely compare myself to others. Instead, I stay focused on myself and my improvement.	1	2	3	4	5

Live and Let Go

25. I can let go of mistakes or failures quickly after learning from them.	1	2	3	4	5
26. I am compassionate with myself, recognizing that everyone, including me, experiences difficulties.	1	2	3	4	5
27. I believe I can grow and change for the better.	1	2	3	4	5

Choose Your Courage Zone

28. I like to try new things and regularly do things that are hard or difficult.	1	2	3	4	5
29. I do things I am afraid of and regularly get out of my comfort zone.	1	2	3	4	5
30. I have big dreams and goals that I am moving forward with courageously.	1	2	3	4	5

Charting your 10 Practices Effectiveness

Total your points for each practice above. Mark each score in the grid below. The higher the score, the more likely you live and perform the 10 Practices. You can go through the workbook starting with Practice 1, or identify the practices you scored lowest on and start with them.

10 Practices Total										
	1	2	3	4	5	6	7	8	9	10
Outstanding 15										
14										
13										
Very Good 12										
11										
10										
Good 9										
8										
7										
Fair 6										
5										
4										
Poor 3										
2										
1										

Get Gritty

The world's best
know what they want and
they know why they want it.
In the face of adversity and setbacks,
they go after their goals with
deep commitment.

When you are gritty,

you have the inner strength and motivation to keep going when it is difficult.

Get Gritty

"Grit is having stamina. Grit is sticking with your future, day in and day out—not just for a day, not just for a month, but for years—to make that future a reality."
—Angela Lee Duckworth

Grit is the quality of sheer persistence. Raw talent can open all sorts of doors for you within your field, but talent alone won't place you among the truly *great*. To be great, you have to know exactly what your long-term goals are. You need to have the reasons for why you're pursuing those goals always in your mind. You have to stick with those goals through setbacks, failure, and adversity, confident that your struggle is meaningful no matter the setbacks.

Grit applies to so much more than just your career. Your education, your relationships, your hobbies, your happiness—all these require vision, passion, and perseverance to truly excel. You'll encounter hardships in each of these areas; only if you're prepared to keep fighting against the tide will you reach your fullest triumph.

Some people may think grit is an inborn quality, but the truth is *anyone* can be gritty. It takes is a knowledge of your goals and of yourself, a roadmap for the future, and the will and inner strength to carry on no matter what. Go the extra mile, trusting it will make a difference—the world's best all know that sustained performance is ultimately what leads to success.

Grit—knowing your long-term goals, knowing why you are pursuing them, and sticking with them—creates success over and beyond talent.

Grit Exercise 1: Get Clear on Your Vision

A vision helps us stay gritty and is the first step in helping us set goals. We *all* need a vision for our future, and once we get clear on our vision, we can make intentional decisions every day. When we have a clear vision, we know what to say "yes" to and what to say "no" to. We can align our daily decisions with it. When we're clear on our vision, we know which opportunities to pursue, which people we need in our midst, and which ideas deserve more attention. But we can't make our vision a reality without clarity.

Most people's visions and dreams are too small. We often let our minds and limiting beliefs get in our way. But when we dream one step more than we normally would, we grow. We are forced to push ourselves. Dreaming above your comfort zone requires you to consider all the possibilities. Today, instead of thinking small, take your vision for your future up a notch.

Step 1. Pick a date five, ten, or twenty years from now to guide the vision exercise. Write that date here:

_____

Step 2. Reflect on the following questions. Picture your life in detail. Go big! What does your future look like on that date?

_____

_____

_____

_____

_____

_____

What have your accomplished by that date?

_____

_____

_____

_____

_____

_____

How do you feel about your life, career, family, and/or sport?

_____

_____

_____

_____

Step 3. Write your vision in a statement below—do so in an active voice, as if it has already happened. Complete the following prompt, starting with the date and adding your response to the questions above:

"On _____ (date of vision), I will be _____

_____,

will have accomplished _____

_____

_____,

and will feel _____

_____."

Step 4. Now imagine your life if you decided to NOT move forward to this new vision. How will it impact your future and the future of others in your life, such as your family, team, or clients, if you decide NOT to move forward with your vision?

_____

_____

_____

_____

Step 5. Share your vision with two people this week who support you in your journey. Secrets rarely come true, so don't keep your vision a secret! What was it like to share your vision with two people? Reflect below.

_____

_____

_____

_____

We all need a vision for our future—once we get clear on our vision, we can make intentional decisions every day.

Grit Exercise 2: Plan Your Destiny

You have now created your compelling vision, and it should make you want to excitedly get of bed each morning. You dreamed big. Now, let's go one step further and turn your vision and big dreams into goals. While a vision inspires you and provides life-changing passion, goals are a vision with deadlines. Goals turn your vision into actions so you can make your vision a reality.

The bottom line is that when you set effective goals, they help you perform up to your potential. Most people think about vague goals, but few know how to set goals that sustain motivation and provide direction (see the Six Gritty Goal Guidelines). You need to write your goals down so you have direction in your performance and in your life.

Step 1. *What do I want to accomplish, have, create, or provide for others in the next 25 years?* Write it all out here. It should be a long list. Fill the next several pages.

_____

_____

_____

_____

_____

_____

_____

_____

Step 2. Next to each goal from the list above, indicate if that goal is a 1-, 3-, 5-, 10-, 20-, or 25-year goal by putting the corresponding number (a 1, 3, 5, 10, 20, 25) in front of the goal.

Step 3. Then pick three or four goals to focus on this year. Write each goal below with as many specific details as possible. Then, write the "why" powering that goal.

1. _____

_____

_____

_____

What's your "why" powering this goal?

_____

_____

2. _____

_____

_____

_____

What's your "why" powering this goal?

_____

_____

3. _____

_____

_____

_____

What's your "why" powering this goal?

_____

_____

4. _____

_____

_____

_____

What's your "why" powering this goal?

_____

_____

Step 4. Next, record the specific actions you can take to move forward toward your goals. Think about how you can close the gap from where you are now to where you intend to go.

_____

_____

_____

_____

_____

_____

_____

_____

_____

_____

_____

_____

_____

_____

_____

_____

Remember, you will always hear that your dreams and goals are unrealistic, impossible, or ill-timed. Choose not to listen.

Grit Exercise 3: No Grit, No Pearl

Think of your life as a pearl. The price of a single pearl on a necklace or ring can range from the low hundreds to tens of thousands of dollars. Pearls are valuable in part because they take years to develop. Did you know that while a small pearl takes around two or three years to grow, it can take a large pearl up to ten years? A pearl starts with a single irritation—a piece of sand, grit, or shell that serves as a parasite inside the oyster. Because of that irritation, the oyster builds layers and layers of calcium carbonate around the piece of grit or sand. The result? A valuable pearl.

Step 1. What are the pearls you want to create? Consider the list of goals from Exercise 2. What are the 2-3 most meaningful on that list? List them below.

_____

_____

_____

_____

_____

Step 2. What sacrifices will you need to make to get the pearl you seek? Indicate those sacrifices below.

_____

_____

_____

_____

Without grit, a pearl is not possible.

Grit Exercise 4: Difficulties Happen for You

There's typically no gain without struggle. Period. When you think about your life and where you're going, remember that losses, failures, setbacks, and challenges are often required to reach your destination. The world's best see that the difficulties that occur can lead them on the course necessary for success. Difficulties show you how strong you are, how persistent you are. They help you understand your true potential and power.

Step 1. How did a problem or difficulty you experienced in the past happen *for* you, not *to* you? How did it lead you to success or where you are today? How did it help you understand yourself and what is important to you?

_____

_____

_____

_____

_____

Step 2. Consider how a second problem or difficulty you experienced in the past happened *for* you, not *to* you. How did it lead to you to success or where you are today?

_____

_____

_____

_____

_____

_____

Step 3. Take at least one problem you're experiencing right now and choose to view it as a puzzle. How does this give you energy or change your perception?

_____

_____

_____

_____

_____

Step 4. What difficulties may you experience _en route_ to your pearls? How do you commit to viewing these difficulties?

_____

_____

_____

_____

_____

The first step in becoming more persistent is to see the difficulties you experience as having happened not to destroy you, but in order to show you how persistent you are.

Grit Exercise 5: Daily Grit Focus Session

The only way to live out your planned destiny and perform at your best is to rule your day: to get organized and disciplined with your actions and habits. You have to concentrate every day on what it takes to become your very best and then exert the discipline and self-control necessary to do what you need to do. Self-control is like a muscle: the more you train it, the stronger it becomes. Each day, you need to resist the things that take you from your goals and vision for your life, staying focused on the things that truly matter.

But how? Start your day with a Grit Focus Session: Take five minutes each morning to reflect on your daily goals and how they relate to your long-term goals. Then, plan out your day in 15-minute segments. This daily habit reminds you of where you are going and why, building your grit and inspiring you to live in an intentional way. It also helps you stay focused throughout your day. Remember to remind yourself of why you want to achieve those goals and dreams to keep you fueled and passionate. You could couple this exercise with mindfulness meditation to make it even more powerful. On the next page, you'll find a worksheet to guide your Daily Grit Focus Session. You can download a PDF to complete each morning at beyondgrit.com/bonus.

Remember, greatness and high performance take intention and daily dedication.

GRIT FOCUS SESSION

TODAY'S DATE:

MY LONG-TERM GOALS: TODAY'S GOALS:

"MY WHY" POWERING THESE GOALS:

6-6:15am	2-2:15pm
6:15-6:30am	2:15-2:30pm
6:30-6:45am	2:30-2:45pm
6:45-7am	2:45-3pm
7-7:15am	3-3:15pm
7:15-7:30am	3:15-3:30pm
7:30-7:45am	3:30-3:45pm
7:45-8:00am	3:45-4pm
8-8:15am	4-4:15pm
8:15-8:30am	4:15-4:30pm
8:30-8:45am	4:30-4:45pm
8:45-9am	4:45-5pm
9-9:15am	5-5:15pm
9:15-9:30am	5:15-5:30pm
9:30-9:45am	5:30-5:45pm
9:45-10am	5:45-6:00pm
10-10:15am	6-6:15pm
10:15-10:30am	6:15-6:30pm
10:30-10:45am	6:30-6:45pm
10:45-11am	6:45-7pm
11-11:15am	7-7:15pm
11:15-11:30am	7:15-7:30pm
11:30-11:45am	7:30-7:45pm
11:45-12pm	7:45-8pm
12-12:15pm	8-8:15pm
12:15-12:30pm	8:15-8:30pm
12:30-12:45pm	8:30-8:45pm
12:45-1pm	8:45-9pm
1-1:15pm	9-9:15pm
1:15-1:30pm	9:30-9:45pm
1:30-1:45pm	9:45-10pm
1:45-2pm	

Remember to Include My Thrive Practices (exercise, meditation, eating well, etc.)

HIGH PERFORMANCE POWER PHRASE:
I rule my day. I am disciplined with my time and daily activities.
Each day I live intentionally and fully engaged.

www.CindraKamphoff.com

Download a PDF of this image at BeyondGrit.com/Bonus

Practice 1
CONCLUDING THOUGHTS

Look! You are on your way to reaching your goals and dreams. Here are the things you did in Get Gritty:

- You wrote down your vision to gain clarity and excitement for your future.

- You recorded your goals (5-, 10-, 20-, and 25-year goals) to get clear on where you're going.

- You considered the pearls you want to create in your life.

- You got clear on your Daily Grit Focus Session.

Now, take a moment to record the following on your Grit Board:

- Your vision for the future.

- A few long-term goals (such as 10-, 20-, or 25-year goals).

- Your 1-year goals.

- The pearls you want to create in your life.

- The phrase "Difficulties happen *for* me, not *to* me."

My High Performance Power Phrase

I am gritty. I do all the things that others are not willing to do to reach my dreams and goals. I put in the hours necessary for success.

2

Get Clear on Your Purpose

The world's best ____ own why they do what they do. They keep their why front and center. This purpose keeps them motivated and hungry when the going gets tough.

Your purpose is your inner guide that helps you choose how to act and think. To get to the next level of your performance, you need to get clear on your purpose.

Get Clear on Your Purpose

"The two most important days in your life are the day you were born, and the day you find out why." —Mark Twain

When things get tough, the world's best don't focus on their worries and frustrations, their hardships and setbacks. They keep their minds fixed on the one thing that matters: their purpose.

Your purpose is unique to you. It's not simply your job description—executive, athlete, parent, spouse, friend. It's the thing that ignites your desire and passion, the objective that makes you come alive when you're working toward its fulfillment. No one else has the same mix of experiences, knowledge, values, gifts, and dreams as you. No one else can offer the world exactly what you can.

Knowing your purpose is key to remaining gritty. Without it, you can get off track, burn out, and forget why you're doing what you're doing in the first place. Your purpose gives you a spark when you want to give up, and reminds you of why you must stay persistent no matter the setback. So ask yourself: What am I fighting for? What makes me want to get up every morning? What lights a fire in my belly? What we can be, we must be. When we reach self-actualization, we thrive and perform at our best more consistently. Our worlds are incomplete until we understand our purpose.

Identifying your purpose and then honoring your purpose is perhaps the most important step that you will make toward high performance!

Exercise 1: Own Your Why

The truth is that few people think extensively about why they do what they do. But when you own your why, things start changing for you. You attract the right people to your business and team, and you get the support you need. When you own your why, you stay fueled and energized, and find more inspiration and a stronger sense of purpose for what you do. You recognize you can get through any difficulty or adversity because of what drives you. Tough days get easier.

So in order to think like the world's best, you need to plug into your bigger purpose and own it. Consider how what you do and want to do helps, inspires, or provides for the people and places that are important to you. It is easier to stay fueled when you know how you contribute to the lives of others. Then, decide to "Own Your Why" daily.

Step 1. Write down what you do—what job or role do you perform? This might be Vice President of Company X, professional basketball player for Y team, or business owner of Company Z.

_____

_____

_____

_____

_____

Step 2. Consider why you do what you do. Think about the good that comes from what you do. Consider the ripples you create when you do good work. How does what you do impact the people around you, your community, and the world? Answer the prompt "So that . . ." six times.

I Do What I Do:

So that _____

_____

So that _____

_____

So that _____

_____

So that _____

_____

So that _____

_____

So that _____

_____

Step 3. Place a star by the most important "So that . . ." answers above.

Step 4. Now, write your "Why" in a single sentence below, reflecting on your "So that . . ." answers from above.

_____

_____

_____

_____

_____

Step 5. Consider how you can "Own Your Why."

Owning your why involves three steps:

1. Communicating your "why" to your clients, family, and friends

2. Using your "why" to inform daily decisions such as what to say "no" and "yes" to

3. Reminding yourself of your "why" daily

In what ways will you commit to "Owning Your Why"?

_____

_____

_____

_____

_____

_____

_____

Everyone has a unique why. Without a clear connection to your why, you can get off track, burn out, and forget to make your why a priority.

Exercise 2: Find Your Fight

You are way too important to just be going through your day and life without passion, purpose, and full engagement. Ask yourself, "What am I fighting for?" For example, I am fighting for the relevance and growth of the field of sport and performance psychology, and the opportunities for women in my field. When I discuss this question with my clients, I see them become more passionate about their work or sport, their team, and their goals. It reflects in their facial expressions and in their body language. Today, dig deep—consider your desires and what you are fighting for. Knowing what you are fighting for will keep your head in the game.

Step 1. What are you fighting for?

_____

_____

_____

_____

_____

_____

_____

Step 2. What if you found out that you had only had six months to live? What would be in your plans? Are they the same or different from what you've planned right now? If not, record the changes you commit to making today.

_____

_____

_____

_____

_____

_____

_____

_____

Step 3. Lastly, how can you remind yourself of what you are fighting for every day? You could remind yourself as you are walking to practice, driving to work, or entering your home. Record below how you will remind yourself of what you are fighting for daily.

_____

_____

_____

_____

_____

_____

**I find my fight. I remind myself every day what I am fighting for.
I stay purposeful and passionate about my life,
work, and family.**

Exercise 3: Write Your Purpose Statement

We've all met people in our lives who inspire us. We remember them. They stood out because they were committed to something bigger. They knew and used their purpose to guide their thinking and actions.

We all have a purpose, and our purpose gives us a reason to persevere. It gives us courage and reminds us of our significance. Your purpose statement is your inner guide that helps you choose how to act and think. When you live on purpose, you know who you are and you bring your whole self to your life intentionally. Living on purpose is a choice we make each day.

Step 1. Reflect on the four questions below to begin to write your purpose statement:

1. What are three words that describe me at my best?

_____

_____

_____

_____

2. What do I want to create or do for myself and others?

_____

_____

_____

_____

3. What is the result or value I provide?

_____

_____

_____

_____

_____

_____

_____

4. Who do I want to help, guide, or inspire in this world?

_____

_____

_____

_____

_____

_____

_____

Step 2. Fill in the blanks below to write the first draft of your purpose statement while considering the six guidelines in the box above.

The purpose of my life is to _____

(use your answer to the first purpose question here),

to _____

(use your answer to the second question here),

and to _____

(use your answer to the third purpose question here)

for _____

(use your answer to the fourth purpose question here).

Step 3. Look at the purpose statement you created and ask yourself if, deep down, you know this is why you do what you do. If it is, yippy! You have an incredible first draft of your purpose statement. If it isn't, play with the words or structure until it is. Replace words that don't get you stoked with ones that do. Write your revised version of your purpose statement below.

_____

_____

_____

_____

_____

Step 4. As a part of your morning routine, say your purpose statement out loud to stay focused and gritty. Post your purpose statement by your bed, on your Grit Board, or by your computer so you see it daily.

Our purpose takes our why one step further. Our purpose takes us deeper into the meaning of our lives and why we are here.

Exercise 4: Identify Your Zone of Genius

In his book *The Big Leap*, Dr. Gay Hendricks describes the activities in our lives as taking place in four zones. Here is a quick summary of the zones:

First Zone: Zone of Incompetence	Activities you are just not good at; other people can do these activities so much better than you. You should avoid these activities because they drain you.
Second Zone: Zone of Competence	Activities that you do well but others can do just as well. You can spend too much time here because while these activities don't drain your energy, they don't provide ultimate fulfillment.
Third Zone: Zone of Excellence	Activities you do extremely well. Even though you do these activities well, this zone can trap you because the activities are in your comfort zone. You are not yet where you are meant to be; therefore, these activities don't allow you to flourish.
Fourth Zone: Zone of Genius	Activities you were uniquely designed to do. You love these things and do the best at them. If you ignore urges to perform these activities, you can experience a loss of direction, conflicts, and depression. You fail to thrive.

The only zone in which you thrive consistently is your Zone of Genius. Your Zone of Genius includes the activities that you were uniquely designed to do. They are the things that you do the best and love. To help you think about what is in—and out of —your Zone of Genius, reflect on these questions:

Step 1. What do you most love to do? (You love it so much you can do it for long stretches of time without getting tired or bored.)

_____

_____

_____

Step 2. What activities do you do that don't seem like work? (Again, you can do them for long stretches of time without getting tired or bored.)

_____

_____

_____

Step 3. What are your unique abilities? What is the special skill you were gifted with?

_____

_____

_____

Step 4. Now, consider your answers to the above three questions. What activities do you think are in your Zone of Genius? What activities do you think you were uniquely designed to do?

_____

_____

_____

Step 5. List the activities that are part of the other Zones that you need to spend less time in:

Zone of Incompetence

_____

_____

Zone of Competence

_____

_____

Zone of Excellence

_____

_____

Step 6. What is an action you can take right now to get closer to living in your Zone of Genius?

_____

_____

_____

**The world's best pay attention and know to stay
in their Zone of Genius.**

Practice 2
CONCLUDING THOUGHTS

Congratulations, my friend! You are one step closer to living and playing with purpose, on purpose. Here are the things you did in Get Clear on Your Purpose:

- You recorded your why and decided to "Own Your Why," which is a game changer.

- You got clear on what you are fighting for.

- You recorded your purpose statement, which is your inner guide that helps you choose how to act and think.

- And you considered the Zone of Genius activities that you were uniquely designed to do.

Now, take a moment to record the following on your Grit Board:

- Your why in a single sentence.

- What you are fighting for.

- Your purpose statement.

- And a few of your Zone of Genius activities.

My High Performance Power Phrase

I live and play on purpose. No one else has the same experiences, knowledge, and gifts that I do. I have a unique purpose and live that purpose.

3

Become a Master of Your Thoughts

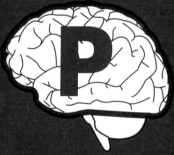

The world's best
are intentional with their self-talk.
They exhibit powerful, positive, and
possibility-oriented thinking patterns
focused on process.

High performers

don't hope their thinking will work for them; they make their thinking work for them. They are intentional and purposeful with their self-talk.

Become a Master of Your Thoughts

"If you think you are beaten, you are. If you think you dare not, you don't. If you'd like to win, but think you can't, it's almost certain you won't." —Walter D. Wintle

We all experience challenging situations. In fact, obstacles and setbacks are a given. It's how we respond to them that matters. When we change how we respond to setbacks, we can maintain our optimism and confidence however dire the circumstance.

What we think about determines everything we do. When we believe our negative thoughts, they affect how we interact with others, how we feel about ourselves, and how we pursue our life goals. If your mind is filled with toxic thoughts, you will act with toxicity. If you want to function at your full potential, you have to learn to master your thinking.

Train your mind to always aid you in reaching for your goals. Be intentional and purposeful; think thoughts that are powerful, possibility-focused, positive, and focused on the process. Your mind simply becomes what you tell it the most. What you think about, you create. What you think about yourself, you become. If you remember to not believe everything you think and focus on the thoughts that make you want to do great things, you'll have made a huge step in achieving and maintaining grittiness.

The world's best athletes, leaders, business people, and entrepreneurs don't believe everything they think. You, my friend, should not believe everything you think either!

Exercise 1: The OPP Strategy

According to research by Martin Seligman, the father of positive psychology, optimists are more likely to live longer, suffer fewer infectious diseases, maintain better health habits, perform more consistently, stress less, and experience more self-confidence and resilience. Optimism decreases the bad and increases the good. To practice optimism on a regular basis, use the Three OPP Strategy: when presented with a difficulty, you identify three opportunities. The Three OPP Strategy helps you expect that something good will come from everything. This strategy helps you stay excited, passionate, and gritty.

Step 1. Write down a difficulty you are experiencing right now. Maybe you lack focus during your game, your company is not positioned to meet its financial goals this year, or your kid is misbehaving at home.

_____

_____

_____

_____

Step 2. Consider at least three opportunities that come from this difficulty. Perhaps this difficulty provides an opportunity for you to learn techniques to improve your focus, to hire additional staff, to spend more time with your child, or to simply focus on the things that are going well instead of dwelling on the things that aren't. Consider the opportunities from that difficulty.

Opportunity 1:

_____

_____

_____

Opportunity 2:

_____

_____

_____

Opportunity 3:

_____

_____

_____

Step 3. Consider how you can use the OPP Strategy daily and who you could share the strategy with to keep you passionate, gritty, and optimistic.

_____

_____

_____

We can change how we see difficulties, obstacles, and setbacks, and in turn, we can maintain our optimism and confidence.

Exercise 2: Identifying your ANTS

We all have negative thoughts. They are called automatic negative thoughts, or ANTs for short, as Dr. Daniel Amen states in his book *Change Your Brain, Change Your Life*. We don't always choose our thoughts, but they drive everything we do. Everything.

Our thoughts determine how we interact with others, how we feel about ourselves, and how we act. Thoughts become emotions that lead to actions and then become habits. Simply put, our thoughts determine our destiny. Too many ANTs deteriorate our ability to perform under pressure and show up as our authentic self.

An important part of reaching your greater potential is recognizing that you shouldn't believe everything you hear—especially in your own mind. Identifying and noticing your ANTs is the first step in controlling your mind before it controls you.

Step 1. To help you gain awareness of your thoughts, circle the ANTs in the table below that you are most likely to think. Commit to taking command of those ANTs.

"Always/Never" Thinking	We use words like *no one, everyone, every time, everything, never,* and *always* out loud or in our minds.
Focusing on the Negative in a Situation	This happens when we see only the bad in a situation and not the good.
Fortune Telling	When we fortune tell, we can predict the worst possible outcome of a situation.
Mind Reading	We mind read when we believe we know what other people are thinking.
Guilt Tripping	Guilt can result from using words like *should, must, have to,* or *ought to.*
Mind Reading	We mind read when we believe we know what other people are thinking.
Personalization	We personalize when we believe negative events have personal meaning.
Labeling	This happens when we attach a negative label to others or ourselves.

Blaming	This happens when you blame someone else for your problems or the situation.

Step 2. To help you recognize the ANTs that hold you back, list the thoughts you often have that don't serve you or lead you to play or live small.

_____

_____

Step 3. List several thoughts that counteract those ANTs listed above. These are thoughts that you know to be true when you look deeply at yourself and your potential.

_____

_____

Thinking that Leads to Your Potential	Thinking that Limits Your Potential
Powerful: A thought that makes you want to do something and move forward toward your big future.	*Defeating:* A thought that makes you feel unworthy, defeated, worn out, or tired.
Possibility-oriented: A thought that allows you to dream about your future and visualize what you want to happen.	*Restrictive:* A thought that causes you to believe things are impossible and settle for average.
Process-focused: A thought that is focused on the present moment and the things you need to do to be at your best.	*Outcome-focused:* A thought that is focused on the outcome, score, or victory, which creates pressure, anxiety, and heaviness.
Positive: A thought that is focused on what you want to happen, including statements that start with "I will . . ."	*Negative:* A thought that is focused on what you want to avoid, including statements that start with "Don't . . ."

For you to experience high performance, your self-talk should be powerful, possibility-oriented, process-focused, and positive. The best of the best experience these thoughts—or P4 thoughts—more often. Research shows that when we have pre-planned, specific thoughts to address our negative thinking, we do a better job at eliminating the negativity than when we just try not to think negatively. Therefore, identify a thought for each of the Ps that you know to be true about yourself that you could say to address your ANTs. Commit today to make P4 Thinking your new standard!

A Powerful Thought:

_____

_____

A Possibility-Oriented Thought:

_____

_____

A Process-Focused Thought:

_____

_____

A Positive Thought:

_____

_____

The world's best athletes and business people think differently than those who experience less success. The best of the best experience P4 thoughts more often.

Exercise 3: Identify Your Power Phrases

If you don't train your mind, you are letting your thoughts happen by chance. Chance thinking does not lead to success. Training your mind takes consistent and daily effort; it is not automatic. In fact, the world's best athletes, leaders, and business people will tell you they have learned to master their thinking. They place deliberate energy and focus on mastering the six inches between their ears.

This is important—our thinking is the most important factor in our success, but we are not typically taught how to think like the most successful people around us. Sometimes we are never taught how to think at all—not by our parents, teachers, or mentors. Instead, we figure it out by trial and error. But there is a better way to learn something than by trial and error.

A powerful way to talk to yourself is to choose Power Phrases. Power Phrases combat destructive phrases such as "I won't . . . ," "I can't . . . ," and "I am not . . ." Rather, they begin with "I will . . . ," "I can . . . ," or "I am . . ."

CHANCES OF SUCCESS

0% I WON'T	60% I MIGHT
10% I CAN'T	70% I WILL
20% I DON'T KNOW HOW	80% I CAN
30% I WISH I COULD	90% I AM
40% I WANT TO	
50% I THINK I MIGHT	

Instead of listening to the ANTs, talk to yourself using "I will . . . I can . . . I am . . ." Power Phrases. Identify Power Phrases below that you know to be true about yourself; then make "I will . . . ," "I can . . . ," and "I am . . ." statements your standard for how you talk to yourself daily.

Step 1. **"I will . . ." is a statement about a positive change or intention.** When you think "I will . . ." you are focusing on what you want and what you intend to make happen. "I will . . ." predicts your future success. Write three "I will . . ." statements below.

1. _____

   _____

   _____

2. _____

   _____

   _____

3. _____

   _____

   _____

Step 2. **"I can . . ." is a statement about your potential.** It is a positive statement about your ability to accomplish your goals and dreams. When you think "I can . . ." you focus on your belief in your ability to do something. Write three "I can . . ." statements below.

1. _____

   _____

   _____

2. _____

   _____

   _____

3. _____

_____

_____

Step 3. **"I am . . ." is the most powerful power phrase because it is a statement about who you are.** The phrase "I am . . ." has the ability to shape your reality and your destiny. When you think "I am . . ." you focus on traits that you already have inside you. Write three "I am . . ." statements below.

1. _____

_____

_____

2. _____

_____

_____

3. _____

_____

_____

When you have your thoughts planned out, you have a plan for eliminating the ANTs and can talk to yourself, not listen.

Exercise 4: Reframe Your Way
Back on Your Game

The world is what we make it, so we can change our lens any time. Reframing helps us to stay stoked and excited despite hardships, no matter how awful things might feel in the moment. When we reframe, we change our viewpoint. Reframing doesn't require that we ignore the injury, difficulty, or pain. Instead, it allows us to see our circumstance differently. How can you challenge the beliefs or assumptions underlying how you see the "negative" event? What is another way of looking at it, an alternate lens? How can you stand in another frame and see a different perspective? All of the negative events and obstacles are helping you learn more about yourself, your situation, and your desire to reach your goals.

To help you reframe, consider three setbacks, difficulties, or challenges you are experiencing right now. Then, shift your perspective and view the situation with a different, reframed lens. Finally, consider how reframing changes how you feel about the difficulty.

Difficulty #1:

_____

Your Reframed Perspective:

_____

_____

How does Reframing Change How You Feel?

_____

_____

Difficulty #2:

_____

Your Reframed Perspective:

_____

_____

How does Reframing Change How You Feel?

_____

_____

Difficulty #3:

_____

Your Reframed Perspective:

_____

_____

How does Reframing Change How You Feel?

_____

_____

You can leverage your grit by reframing to remain excited, passionate, and on track even when a circumstance, challenge, or tragedy throws you off your path.

Exercise 5: The CAR Shift

We all can needlessly, passively, endlessly, and excessively ponder the meanings, causes, or consequences of things. We can overthink anything: our athletic performance, our success, our failure, our families, our appearance, our career, or our health. Overthinking is a serious problem because we cannot perform at our highest level when we engage in it. Overthinking interferes with our problem-solving skills, zaps our motivation, impairs our ability to think like the world's best, fosters ANTs, and prevents us from pursuing our goals. Overthinking gives us a distorted, pessimistic view of our life. It can feel like quicksand!

To help reduce overthinking, I've outlined a three-step process. I call this process the CAR Shift. CAR helps you shift gears in your mind instead of in your car. Using the CAR Shift can help you make your thinking more productive.

Practice the CAR Shift below:

"C" is for Catch it.

The key is to "catch" or notice the thought. Self-awareness moment-to-moment will help you identify when negative thoughts impact your mood and body. Identify at least one thought that limits your future below:

_____

_____

_____

_____

_____

"A" is for Address it.

Don't let negativity grow. Decide to address and confront it head on. You have two choices in addressing the ANTs: either talk back to the ANT, providing evidence on why your thought is not accurate or true, or let the thought move out of your mind like a cloud. Identify how you will address the ANT below:

_____

_____

_____

_____

"R" is for Refocus it.

To get out of your head, refocus on the next step to reach your goals. What is the next thing you need to do to move forward? What do you want to focus on externally instead? Identify how you will refocus your attention below:

_____

_____

_____

_____

The world's best are intentional with their self-talk.

CONCLUDING THOUGHTS

Wow! You are continuing to make progress toward thinking like the world's best!

Here are the things you did in Be a Master of Your Thinking.

- You outlined the OPP Strategy and chose to think like an optimist.

- You recorded the Automatic Negative Thoughts or ANTs that you are most likely to think.

- You got clear on how to reframe your difficulties, setbacks, or challenges.

- You identified your Power Phrases.

Now, take a moment to record the following on your Grit Board:

- 4 P4 Thoughts you want to say to yourself regularly.

- Your 3 Power Phrases to use daily.

- An example of your new reframe or your CAR Shift.

My High Performance Power Phrase

I talk to myself, not listen. I think "I will . . . I can . . . I am . . ." to help me reach my wicked awesome potential.

4

Know Yourself to Master Yourself

SUCCESS

What people think it looks like   What it really looks like

The world's best understand themselves and their tendencies, and are in tune with their thoughts, emotions, and actions. They know they need to master themselves to be successful.

People or situations

don't make us feel a certain way. Instead, we choose how to think, feel, and respond.

Know Yourself to Master Yourself

"Awareness is the greatest agent for change." —Eckhart Tolle

Self-awareness is the foundation of our ability to deal with challenges and adversity. When we are self-aware, we know ourselves—what we do well, how we can improve, what jazzes us, and what people or situations push our buttons. Athletes, leaders, and business people who are self-aware can accurately perceive their emotions in a nonjudgmental way. A nonjudgmental awareness is key in your journey to reach the next level and think like the world's best.

When you are self-aware, you understand yourself, pursue your passion (instead of someone else's), and don't let emotions like fear and anxiety hold you back. People or situations don't make us feel a certain way—we choose how to feel and what we do. Without self-awareness, you can lose that control, overwhelmed with anxiety, doubt, and frustration. With it, you and only you dictate your response to whatever life throws your way. You can act with purpose and intention regardless of challenges or setbacks.

If negative thoughts start to eat away at you, take a step back. Make sure that your thoughts are centered in the present moment, motivated and determined, and always defined by your ultimate goals and purpose. You'll be one step closer to owning your future.

Take a huge step toward your awesome, gritty future by moving forward with increased self-awareness.

Exercise 1: My MVP Level

Think about someone who has earned the title of "MVP" (or Most Valuable Player) of their team or a league. They couldn't have earned that title without knowing what leads to their personal best—or their MVP level—and consistently understanding their mind. You cannot perform at your MVP level—your personal best—if you are not using your mind in a productive way. Every decision goes through your mind; the key is to keep your mind working for you, not against you. You can't perform at your MVP level without understanding what led you to consistently performing at that level.

When you are at your best, you have no regrets because you are giving your life and sport your all. There is nothing that you would change because you gave all that you could. Your MVP level is meaningful, fulfilling, and fun.

Let's consider what it means for you to be at your MVP Level.

Step 1. Think about a time when you were at your MVP level. What thoughts, feelings, and actions led you to be at your best? What did your body feel and look like?

_____

_____

_____

_____

_____

_____

_____

Step 2. Think about a time you were not at your best or when you performed poorly. What thoughts, feelings, and actions led to this performance? What did your body feel and look like? Were there any distractions or uncontrollable factors that you were focused on?

_____

_____

_____

_____

_____

Step 3. Compare and contrast your lists from Steps 1 and 2. What led to you being at your best? What did not? What are the biggest differences between the lists?

_____

_____

_____

_____

_____

Step 4. To get more clear on your MVP level:

- Circle five emotions from the list below that lead to your MVP level. Remember that even emotions that we might consider negative may help you to be at your best.

- Then, put a box around five emotions from the list below that hinder your performance and do not lead you to your MVP level.

Angry	Anxious	Happy	Confident	Nervous	Dissatisfied
Tired	Depressed	Energetic	Charged	Easygoing	Fearless
Uncertain	Unwilling	Lazy	Sluggish	Brisk	Alert
Overjoyed	Quiet	Motivated	Calm	Loose	Wired
Engaged	Hostile	Annoyed	Aggressive	Frustrated	Resentful
Doubtful	Incapable	Fatigued	Self-absorbed	Fearful	Crushed
Aching	Agitated	Free	Connected	Accepting	Friendly
Present	Humble	Gentle	Eager	Absorbed	Amazed
Hopeful	Resourceful	Reliable	Pleased	Balanced	Grateful
Focused	Judgmental	Kind	Optimistic	Courageous	Flexible
Tense	Animated	Satisfied	Irritated	Furious	Rejected

Step 5. Consider what specific actions you can take before or during your day or performance to experience your MVP level more consistently.

_____

_____

_____

_____

We are more likely to thrive, experience achievement and success, and advance to the next level when we perform with emotions that support our MVP level.

Exercise 2: Find Your Flow

When you experience flow, you are using your skills to their fullest and are so absorbed in the task that nothing else matters. You feel effortless. You are performing at your best. You can experience flow in any activity you enjoy: flow is the ultimate optimal experience.

Psychologist Mihaly Csikszentmihalyi, the author of bestselling book *Flow: The Psychology of Optimal Experience*, is considered the grandfather of flow, the first to coin the term. He describes ten core components to flow. Flow is possible when the challenge of what you are doing and the demands of the situation match, along with nine other components.

Csikszentmihalyi suggested there are ten core components to flow including:

- A balance between skill and challenge

- Immediate feedback

- Clear goals

- Action and awareness merging

- High concentration on the task at hand

- A sense of control

- A loss of self-consciousness

- A transformation of time

- The activity is intrinsically motivating or what is called "autotelic"

- Absorption in the task

When you experience a few of these components, it's microflow. When all of the ten components happen at once, it's macroflow.

Sometimes when I am working with athletes, coaches, and business leaders, they want a magic ticket to get in their flow zone. Unfortunately, flow isn't like a light switch that you can turn on and off. Instead, you can gain awareness by examining your experience in flow, understanding the components that lead to flow, and channeling your focus to the present moment.

Step 1. Think about a time that you were in the flow. How did your flow zone feel? What led to that feeling? What were your expectations and goals before the performance?

_____

_____

_____

_____

_____

Step 2. Contrast this to a time you were not able to focus and you struggled. What were the differences between these times for you? What got in the way of experiencing flow?

_____

_____

_____

_____

_____

Step 3. Looking at the ten core components of flow in the box above, which are you less likely to experience, preventing you from experiencing flow?

_____

_____

_____

_____

_____

_____

Step 4. What mental tools presented in _Beyond Grit_ can you commit to using more often to increase your likelihood of experiencing flow?

_____

_____

_____

_____

_____

_____

Finding your flow zone starts with your mind and channeling your focus to the present moment.

Exercise 3: Respond, Not React

"Between stimulus and response there is a space. In that space, is our freedom and power to choose our response. In our response lies our growth and freedom."
—*Victor Frankl*, Man's Search for Meaning

In his bestselling book *Man's Search for Meaning*, Victor Frankl, a neurologist and psychiatrist, described his experiences as a concentration camp inmate during the Holocaust. In his highly influential book, Frankl said that our life is about how we interpret moments of difficulty and respond to them.

We often react with heightened anxiety, fear, guilt, or doubt, believing that things make us feel this way. We react without thinking. We don't always see that we choose our response. When we react without thinking, we stay stuck where we are without growing. We don't act or think like a high performer. When we are self-aware, we notice what Frankl calls the "space" between the stimulus (what happens) and our response (how we choose to act, think, and feel). We can increase and make use of this space. We can choose to respond and can act with purpose and intention. We can respond not react. To help you increase the space between stimulus and response, reflect on the questions below:

Step 1. Consider a time that you put space between the stimulus and your response and it helped you. What did you do to gain control of your response? How did it feel gaining control?

_____

_____

_____

_____

Step 2. Consider a time that you lost control of your emotions and increasing the space between stimulus and response could have helped you. What happened and how could you have gained control?

_____

_____

_____

_____

_____

_____

_____

Step 3. What are a few times in the past few weeks where increasing the space between stimulus and response could have benefited your performance or happiness?

_____

_____

_____

_____

_____

When you respond not react, you stay gritty, in control, and focused to be a higher performer.

Exercise 4: Master Your Green Light

As Ken Ravizza and Tom Hanson discussed in their book *Heads-Up Baseball: Playing the Game One Pitch at a Time*, think of your body and performance as a traffic light. Green means "go," yellow means "caution," and red means "stop." Unless you are just learning to drive a car, you don't even see the traffic light when it is green. You keep driving. The same is true when you are at your best throughout your day. The green light represents you at your best. You don't need to make adjustments to yourself, your reaction, or your actions. You are thinking, acting, and responding like the world's best.

The yellow light is when you are starting to lose your high-performance mentality. You are just going through the motions, are a little too anxious or tense, or feel rushed. You are in the early stages of losing control or performing unconfidently.

When you experience the red light in your body and performance, you have completely lost the high-performance mentality. You are struggling. You may have lost control of your emotions and your mindset. The key is to regain control of your mind and body as soon as possible; it's easier to regain control after a yellow light than a red one. Choose to pay attention to yourself and make adjustments to think and act like the world's best.

Step 1. Complete a Stoplight Grid to reflect on your green, yellow, and red lights:

In Your Green Light:	In Your Yellow Light:	In Your Red Light:
I am saying to myself:	I am saying to myself:	I am saying to myself:
I am feeling:	I am feeling:	I am feeling:
I am focused on:	I am focused on:	I am focused on:

Step 2. What specific actions or mental tools will you use to move from your yellow or red lights to your green light? List at least two or three you could use. For example, you could use a Power Pause outlined in the box above.

_____

_____

_____

_____

To reach high performance and be at your best consistently, day after day, month after month, year after year, self-awareness is key.

CONCLUDING THOUGHTS

Bravo! Your focus and hard work continues! You are on your way to being aware like a high performer!

Here are the things you did in Know Yourself to Master Yourself:

- You found your MVP level—or your personal best—and considered what you can do to get there consistently.

- You reflected on what leads to flow and how you can experience it more often.

- You considered how you can respond not react.

- And you completed the Stoplight Grid and committed to the mental tools you can use to stay or move to your green light.

Now, take a moment to record the following on your Grit Board:

- 5 words that describe your MVP Level.

- A few key phrases from this section, such as "Respond Not React," "Increase the Space," or "Find My Flow."

- A picture of a stoplight to remind yourself to stay in your green light.

My High Performance Power Phrase
**I work to understand myself and my tendencies.
I master myself to reach a new level.**

5

Dominate the Controllables

The world's best
dominate what they have control over—their attitude,
preparation, and effort—instead
of what they cannot.

When we dominate

our APE, we are showing up in the world, on our team, and with our family as the best version of ourselves.

Dominate the Controllables

"Life is 10 percent of what happens to me and 90 percent of how I respond to it."
—John Maxwell

Life, athletics, and business can be simply divided into two areas: 1) things that you can control, and 2) things you cannot control. In sports, you can't control your teammates; in business, you can't control your competitors; in life, you can't control any of the many people you interact with. When you focus on these uncontrollables, it leads only to frustration, anxiety, and fear. If you want to reach high performance, you need to learn to focus on dominating what *can* be controlled—namely, your own thoughts and actions.

Dominating the controllables—or your attitude, preparation, and effort (APE)—is key to high performance. When you refuse to let your attitude be dictated by external circumstances, you stop anxiety and anger from sinking in. When you make sure to prepare, going above and beyond to be ready for whatever heads your way, you ensure that you're a master of your craft regardless of the obstacles in your path. When you put in your best effort regardless of whether you'll win the day or not, you build up the inner grit that is key to your eventual success.

When we are dominating our APE, we don't let our attention go to things we cannot control even for one minute.

Exercise 1: Dominating Your APE

Uncontrollables, or the things outside the circle in the image below, can take us off our game and further away from reaching our high-performance potential consistently. For every minute we are focused on things we cannot control, we are taking away energy and passion for our goals. We are draining our mindset and passion instead of fueling them.

When we dominate our focus on what we can control, we are more likely to experience high performance. We are more likely to reach our goals and dreams because we are not wasting energy or focus on things we have no control over. We are thinking like the world's best when we are dominating the controllables.

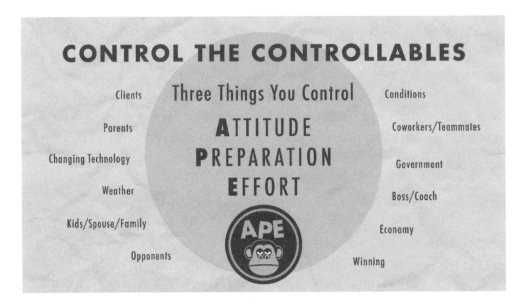

Step 1. Consider what uncontrollables (outside the circle) you tend to focus on. List those factors below to gain awareness.

_____

_____

_____

_____

_____

Step 2. Now, consider what you can do to dominate your APE (attitude, preparation, and effort).

Attitude – What does it look like and feel like when you are completely dominating your attitude?

_____

_____

_____

_____

_____

Preparation – What does it look like and feel like when you are completely dominating your preparation?

_____

_____

_____

_____

_____

Effort – What does it look like and feel like when you are completely dominating your effort?

_____

_____

_____

_____

_____

Step 3. When you are focused on the uncontrollables, follow the three simple steps in the box above. List the phrase you can say to dominate your APE ("Dominate my APE," "APE up," "C & C," or "Control the controllables").

_____

_____

_____

_____

_____

High performers know they control the amount of focus and intensity they use to pursue mastery. When you do your best daily, your best just becomes better.

Exercise 2: Victim and Creator Language

Most of us are conditioned to blame someone else for our suffering. When we blame others, we weaken our power and our ability to be high performers. Every time we blame someone or something, we dwindle our chances of success and reaching our goals. We don't think or act like the world's best. The more we blame others, the less gritty we become.

High performers take responsibility for their past and future. They realize that their choices and decisions led them to where they are today. They accept responsibility for their past but don't dwell in it. They choose to think clearly about themselves and grab ahold of their future. They think and act like creators, not victims.

Victims	Creators
Victims create excuses and blame others. They complain and feel like they "have" to do things. They pretend their problems belong to others. They repeat actions that are ineffective. They seldom reach their goals.	Creators solve problems, take action, and accept responsibility. They *choose* to follow through and own their problems. They commit and take control of their lives. They achieve their goals because they work hard and are gritty.
Victim Language: • "I am overweight because my parents are overweight." • "I was cut from the team because the coach was unfair." • "That's such a stupid requirement." • "He is such as lousy boss." • "It's not my fault that I am late to practice." • "I wish I could run faster."	*Creator Language:* • "I will reclaim my energy by losing weight." • "I will put more effort into developing my skills and ability to make the team." • "I am going to complete this requirement with full effort." • "My boss has a lot of great qualities." • "I was late because I didn't look at my watch." • "I will improve my speed by running twice a week."

Step 1. Take a minute to write down victim statements that you think or say that are not helping you take responsibly for your future.

_____

_____

_____

_____

Step 2. Now, rewrite those victim statements into the language of a creator to generate energy for your gritty future.

_____

_____

_____

_____

Step 3. Write a powerful creator statement you can use to remind yourself to take control of your gritty future:

_____

_____

_____

_____

The world's best know that they are the only person responsible for their quality of life. They look inside and create the life and performance they desire.

Exercise 3: Believe in the Best-Case Scenario

Neuropsychologists found that when your brain expects something to happen, it works to achieve it at a subconscious level. Your expectation creates it. Your brain takes over the job of accomplishing what you see. If you expect the worst, you will get the worst. If you expect the best, you are more likely to get the best. Expectation impacts your behavior, which can cause what we expect to actually happen.

The first step is believing high performance can happen for you. The key is to focus on what you want to happen, not on what you don't want to happen. Only after you believe can you put a plan in place to make it a reality. Instead of focusing on the worst-case scenario, focus on what you want to happen instead. Choose a gritty perspective and shift your thoughts away from the worst-case scenario, instead considering the best-case scenario and what I call the "my-scenario." Your "my-scenario" is what you plan and can create. It focuses on the process, not the outcome, and on what you can control.

Step 1. Consider an important event or performance you have coming up in your life that you want to do well at. Describe it below.

_____

_____

_____

_____

_____

_____

_____

Step 2. Now, describe the worst-case scenario. For example, this could be an outcome you fear.

_____

_____

_____

_____

_____

Step 3. Outline the best-case scenario. If things went perfectly, what would be the outcome?

_____

_____

_____

_____

Step 4. Describe my-scenario. This is a scenario you can control. It is focused on the process (not the outcome) and on the small things you can do.

_____

_____

_____

_____

_____

Step 5. Lastly, outline a plan to implement your my-scenario.

_____

_____

_____

_____

_____

_____

_____

_____

Continually believe in the best-case scenario and make it happen with your my-scenario. This will change your future and bring your grit to a whole new level.

Exercise 4: Design a Contingency Plan

One of my mentors, Dr. Dan Gould (along with his graduate students), has conducted numerous studies examining Olympic teams and athletes, comparing and contrasting those who thrived with those who did not. They found those who succeeded at the Olympics had a plan to deal with distractions and were detailed in their competition plans. They had a contingency plan. They had a plan for the things that might get in the way of being their best. By planning, they were ready for anything and could stay confident, calm, focused, and on their game.

A contingency plan is a plan to deal with the unexpected. A key is to see things that may get in your way as simply "imperfections," to emphasize that they are just blemishes or undesirable features. They are not problems, just imperfect things happening around you. When you plan for imperfections, you have a back-up plan ready and can stay calm and confident. You are prepared.

Step 1. Describe an important event you have coming up in your life.

_____

_____

_____

_____

Step 2. Consider the "imperfections" that could get in the way of an ideal performance. List those below. Then, plan your reaction or strategy. How would you deal with these imperfections?

Imperfection #1:

_____

_____

_____

My planned reaction or strategy:

_____

_____

_____

_____

Imperfection #2:

_____

_____

_____

My planned reaction or strategy:

_____

_____

_____

_____

Imperfection #3

_____

_____

My planned reaction or strategy:

_____

_____

_____

_____

Imperfection #4:

_____

_____

_____

My planned reaction or strategy:

_____

_____

_____

_____

Life, sports, and business are not perfect; therefore, it is best to plan for things that might happen so you are ready for anything and can capitalize on what comes.

Practice 5
CONCLUDING THOUGHTS

You are over halfway through this book! In Dominate the Controllables, you did the following:

- You outlined the controllables—or your APE—to be in control of your destiny.

- You decided to think and act like a creator and outlined your creator language.

- You described a "my-scenario" to dominate the process and what you are in control over.

- And you chose to be fully prepared and designed a contingency plan.

Now, take a moment to record the following on your Grit Board:

- Your APE phrase to say focused on what you can control.

- A creator phrase to help you stay in control of your destiny.

- A few key phrases from this section, such as "I am a Creator!" or "Believe in My-Scenario."

My High Performance Power Phrase

I dominate my APE. I use the 86,400 seconds in my day to develop my knowledge and skills. I give my best attitude, preparation, and effort day in and day out.

Own the Moment

The world's best
stay present-moment focused.
They recognize that they can't control the
past or the future, but they are empowered
to reach their highest potential when they
are engaged in the present moment.

Getting back
to the present moment
is about two practices:
awareness and choice.

Own the Moment

"This is your moment. Own it." —Oprah Winfrey

Mindfulness is choosing to be awake in the moment. It's non-judgmentally being aware of what you are thinking, feeling, and doing. You aren't working to change what is happening around you. You don't work to fight or judge your situation. Instead, you notice and become aware.

When you train yourself to pay attention to your thoughts, feelings, and actions, you'll notice right away what your needs are—more rest, distance from a toxic person or situation, time to center yourself, etc. When you bring your attention back to the moment, it's a relief from stress and the weight of the demands you may be experiencing. A common misconception is that trying harder will lead to success. Truth is, it won't. Over-trying comes when we focus solely on the outcome; we tense up, worry about the past or the future. We simply try too hard. Instead, stay focused on the task—the process—and the small things you need to do to be successful.

When you stay focused on individual steps of the process, you are more likely to persist. It ensures your self-worth isn't directly tied to a certain outcome. You'll think less about failure and what other people think. You'll be thinking like the world's best. When you focus on the process, you put forth your best effort and thus experience high performance more often.

The process is what you do day in and day out to be successful—to think and act like the world's best.

Exercise 1: Attack the Process

When you stay focused daily on the process—the small things you need to do to crush your goals—you are more likely to persist, and persistence and grit are needed to accomplish your goals. You will be more likely to stay passionate about your work and have a higher sense of satisfaction and accomplishment. Focusing on the process will ensure your self-worth isn't directly tied to the results or the outcome. You'll think less about failure and the past. You'll be thinking like the world's best.

To focus on the process, you must break down your goal and relentlessly focus what it takes to get there. In the space below, consider how you can attack and dominate the process.

Step 1. Select an important long-term or one-year goal you wrote down from Practice 1. Record that goal in a specific way below.

_____

_____

_____

_____

_____

_____

Step 2. Outline the steps that are in your control to reach that goal. What is the process needed to get where you want to go?

_____

_____

_____

_____

_____

_____

_____

Step 3. Now consider the daily steps you need to take that will lead to your goal and the extraordinary result. Your daily focus should be on these steps.

_____

_____

_____

_____

_____

_____

_____

_____

Care more about executing the process than the outcome, the score, or your competition. Trust yourself and the process.

Exercise 2: Training Present Moment Focus

Your success is determined by your ability to stay in the present moment. Your mind can be one of three places—the past, the present, or the future. When you are focused on the past, you are more likely to experience negative emotions such as anger, frustration, regret, and depression. When you are focused on the future, you are more likely to experience negative emotions such as fear, anxiety, self-doubt, and pressure. You are more likely to have an outcome-focus over a process-focus when you are focused on the future.

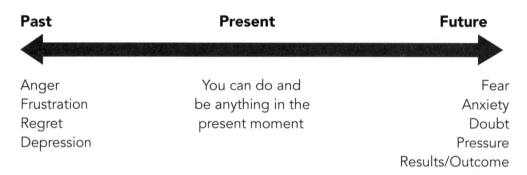

Past	Present	Future
Anger	You can do and	Fear
Frustration	be anything in the	Anxiety
Regret	present moment	Doubt
Depression		Pressure
		Results/Outcome

In the present moment, however, you can do anything you want to. Pressure does not exist. You are focused on the process. The great thing is that you can train your present moment focus. To stay focused on the here and now, commit to staying aware of your focus, moment by moment. It's all about awareness first, choice second.

To help you gain self-awareness and present moment focus, consider the following.

Step 1. Reflect on a time where your mind was focused in the past in a negative way. What was the consequence?

_____

_____

_____

_____

_____

_____

_____

_____

Step 2. Reflect on a time where your mind was focused in the future in a negative way. What was the consequence?

_____

_____

_____

_____

_____

_____

_____

Step 3. Reflect on a time where your mind was focused in the present. What was the benefit?

_____

_____

_____

_____

_____

_____

_____

Step 4. How do you plan to train your present moment focus (see Chapters 28 and 30 in *Beyond Grit* for a discussion)?

_____

_____

_____

_____

_____

_____

_____

No matter the situation, the present moment is the only place your best performance can take place.

Exercise 3: See Pressure as a Privilege

We often see pressure as something we don't want to experience. We avoid it. If we see it as something we want to avoid, we crumble under it, and thereby limit our opportunities and ourselves. Seeing pressure as a threat decreases our self-confidence, increases our fear of failure, and negatively impacts our attention and short-term memory. The world's best see pressure differently. They realize it is impossible to live a life without pressure and instead choose to see pressure as a privilege. The world's best see pressure as a challenge or as an opportunity. They don't avoid pressure; they use it. They reframe it as a good thing.

Hendrie Weisinger and J. P. Pawliw-Fry, in their *New York Times* bestselling book *Performing Under Pressure*, provide three factors that explain why we underperform under pressure:

- The outcome is important to us

- The outcome is uncertain

- We feel that we are responsible for and are being judged on the outcome

Weisinger and J. P. Pawliw-Fry found high-achievers use natural tools within themselves to perform at their best during moments of high pressure. To help think like a high performer, reflect on times you experience pressure and how you can see pressure as a challenge or opportunity in the future.

Step 1. Consider a time in the past you experienced pressure as a threat. What contributed to your seeing pressure in a negative way?

_____

_____

_____

_____

Step 2. How do pressure situations generally make you feel? What thoughts generate those feelings?

_____

_____

_____

_____

_____

Step 3. Write out your concerns about the high-pressure situation you are facing. How can you see this situation and the pressure you are experiencing as a privilege?

_____

_____

_____

_____

_____

Remember the Pressure Principle:
Pressure is a privilege. Pressure allows me to get better. Pressure is an honor. Pressure leads me to greatness. I have earned the right to feel pressure.

Practice 6
CONCLUDING THOUGHTS

You are crushing it! You are well on your way to developing a High Performance Mindset! In Own the Moment, you did the following:

- You attacked the process with one of your outcome goals to stay focused on the process 95 percent of the time.

- You got clear on what happens when you are focused on the past or future in a negative way.

- And you considered how you can see pressure as an opportunity.

Now, take a moment to record the following on your Grit Board:

- 2-3 process goals you want to focus on to stay gritty.

- The pressure principle.

- A few key phrases from this section such as "Awareness First, Choice Second" or "Pressure is a Privilege!"

My High Performance Power Phrase

I live in the moment. I take one play at a time. I can do anything and be anything right here, right now.

7

Choose Empowering Emotions

3:1

The world's best

thrive because they regularly experience
positive emotions. They know that when people
experience three positive emotions for every one
negative emotion, they flourish.

When you choose

happiness, you start committing
to better mental habits,
choose environments that
support your decision,
and are more committed
to reprogramming beliefs
that hold you back.

Practice 7

Choose Empowering Emotions

"The greatest discovery of any generation is that a human can alter his life by altering his attitude." —William James, psychologist

---

Negativity has real implications for your performance. It impacts the culture of your family and team. It impacts your health and your wellness. It impacts every part of your life. However, positivity also has measurable effects. It's pretty clear which one you should be striving for as you pursue your goals.

Many people think that positivity needs to come from an event; "I need to play well, do well, receive a compliment, or be treated well to be positive." But the world's best know this isn't true. Positivity is a choice. Nothing needs to happen for you to be positive. It's a state of mind!

Having skill and talent isn't entough. You need to *choose* to feel good to make it happen. Barbara Fredrickson's groundbreaking book *Positivity: Top-Notch Research Reveals the 3-to-1 Ratio That Will Change Your Life* reveals that we need a ratio of 3 positive emotions to 1 negative emotion to thrive and feel alive. When you choose to feel empowering emotions, you are remarkably resilient. You believe in and are excited about your future. You perform at a high level physically, socially, and psychologically. You celebrate the greatness in others. You are gritty and go after your goals and dreams.

Positivity is a choice. Positivity does not need to come from an event. Nothing needs to happen for you to be positive.

Exercise 1: Choosing Empowering Emotions

One of the first steps in choosing empowering emotions daily is to consider the empowering emotions that you want to feel and the disempowering emotions you don't want to feel. You might feel the disempowering emotions from time to time, but you don't want to get stuck in them. Intentionally making a decision on how you want to feel helps you choose your empowering emotions. There are over 4,000 words to express emotion in the English language, but most people *experience* fewer than a dozen in a given week. In the exercise below, I've provided a few examples of emotions to jump-start your thinking. I encourage you to consider new emotions that you don't typically use to name how you want to feel and expand your emotional range.

Step 1. Write down three empowering or positive emotions you consistently want to feel.

Empowering emotions might include: authentic, blessed, confident, compassionate, courageous, creative, energized, excited, fascinated, grateful, hopeful, happy, loved, inspired, joyful, motivated, optimistic, passionate, proud, smart, or wondrous.

_____

_____

_____

_____

_____

_____

_____

Step 2. Write down three disempowering or negative emotions you don't consistently want to feel.

Disempowering emotions might include: anxious, angry, annoyed, ashamed, confused, depressed, dejected, discouraged, dissatisfied, embarrassed, frustrated, guilty, judged, tired, stressed, weak, worried, or worthless.

_____

_____

_____

_____

_____

_____

Step 3. Identify at least two things you commit to doing every day to choose to feel more empowered emotions and fewer disempowered emotions.

_____

_____

_____

_____

Your mind is a powerful thing. When you fill it with positivity and choose to feel empowered, your life and performance will change.

Exercise 2: Choose Confidence

Having skill and talent isn't enough. You need to *believe* in your own success for it to happen. Confidence is belief and trust in your ability. It is your certainty that you will be successful. If you let your self-confidence get swamped by doubt and anxiety, you'll drift further and further away from the grit that you need to take your performance to the next level.

Confidence requires constant nurturing. Even if you are at the top of your field, sport, or company, nurturing your confidence is key if you want to remain at the top. To develop confidence, consider the ten decisions you can make:

Download a PDF of this image at BeyondGrit.com/Bonus

The most powerful sources of confidence are past performances or achievements. When you have accomplished good things in the past, you are more likely to believe you can do so in the future. Your past accomplishments are tangible evidence that you can do it, because you've already done it! Remind yourself daily of how you have improved your skills over time.

Step 1: Identify an area in your life where you would like to improve your confidence. For example, that may be speaking in front of others or believing you can be successful in your sport.

_____

_____

Now identify three experiences in the past where you have been successful in that area. For example, that could be three times you have been successful speaking in front of others, or three of your best memories in your sport. Provide as many details as you can about each experience in the space below.

Experience 1:

_____

_____

_____

_____

_____

_____

_____

Experience 2:

_____

_____

_____

_____

_____

Experience 3:

_____

_____

_____

_____

_____

When you lack confidence, remind yourself of one of these three experiences. Play that experience through your mind as a highlight reel. It's evidence that you have been successful in the past and can be successful now!

Confidence is a choice you make daily. Intentionally decide today to take control of your confidence. Believe and trust that you can!

Exercise 3: Happiness-Improving Question

Happiness is a choice each of us can make daily, regardless of our circumstances or surroundings. Making a choice to be happy can help us be more productive, live longer, and maintain deeper, lasting relationships. A key part of improving our happiness is improving the questions that we allow to run through our mind. One way to improve our thoughts is to plan the type of questions we ask ourselves so we focus on the opportunity instead of the difficulty or what is right instead of what is wrong.

Examples of Happiness-Improving Questions:

- How is this situation a gift?

- What is amazing about my team?

- What am I happy about right now?

- What is great about my situation?

- What is wonderful about my work?

- What is awesome about my family?

- What is going right in my life?

- What can I be thankful for?

- What progress have I made?

Your Happiness-Improving Questions: In the space provided, identify three happiness-improving questions you could ask yourself regularly. Then put a star by the question you commit to asking yourself every day:

1. _____

   _____

2. _____

_____

_____

_____

3. _____

_____

_____

4. _____

_____

_____

_____

Just by deciding to be happier, you will see an impact. Simply trying to be happier can actually elevate your mood and well-being.

Exercise 4: Choose Gratitude

Gratitude is more than saying "thank you"—it is not taking the small things for granted. We aren't automatically thankful. Gratitude is an intentional practice that heightens our performance and grit. Gratitude is the perfect antidote to negative emotions because it's impossible to feel gratitude at the same time as fear, anxiety, worry, envy, or anger. Gratitude reminds us to appreciate things that can't be scored or counted—things like teamwork, friendship, and improvement.

Tool 1: **Take a gratitude visit.** In the space below, write a note letting one person know you appreciate him or her for what he or she did for you. Notice how writing the note improves your gratitude for that person. Then, cut it out of the book and give it to them, or retype it in an email and send it off!

_____

_____

_____

_____

_____

_____

_____

_____

_____

Tool 2: **Write a birthday gratitude list.** Choose a person you are grateful for or someone you want to be more grateful for (such as a family member, teacher, coach, or friend). Every day this year, write one thing you appreciate about that person below. Give them the list on their next birthday. Here is a place for you to start recording below.

Day 1:	Day 2:	Day 3:	Day 4:	Day 5:	Day 6:
Day 7:	Day 8:	Day 9:	Day 10:	Day 11:	Day 12:
Day 13:	Day 14:	Day 15:	Day 16:	Day 17:	Day 18:
Day 19:	Day 20:	Day 21:	Day 22:	Day 23:	Day 24:
Day 25:	Day 26:	Day 27:	Day 28:	Day 29:	Day 30:

Grateful people use words like *blessed, blessings, fortunate, lucky, abundance, privileged, gifts,* or *givers.*

Exercise 5: Imagery Plan

Imagery involves systematically using your senses to create a past or future event in your mind. Imagery is not just causal daydreaming, but a systematic process of visualizing to improve your performance. It is focused preparation. Imagery is a powerful mental skill and is reportedly used by 99 percent of the world's best. It's so powerful because your mind doesn't know the difference between a vividly imagined event and a real one; your brain uses the same systems for both real and imagined events. In this exercise, create the structure of your personal highlight reel by outlining three excellent past performances, followed by the next time you want to perform your best.

Step 1: Imagine 90 Seconds of Excellent Past Performances

Write about 3 personal highlights in which you performed at your best.

1. _____

   _____

   _____

2. _____

   _____

   _____

3. _____

   _____

   _____

Step 2: Imagine 1 Minute of a Future Performance

Write about how you want to perform in a future occurrence. Pick a time you really want to crush it. Write about how you want to feel and what you want to be thinking. Give as many details as you can.

_____

_____

_____

_____

_____

_____

_____

_____

_____

Now put these steps together. First, imagine your past three performances in about 30 seconds each. Then, conclude your imagery with your future performance. Imagine your highlight reel daily. Remember the VICE acronym to make your imagery come alive.

Include imagery as part of your daily routine. It will help you think like the world's best and accomplish even more than you thought was possible!

Exercise 6: The Five People Exercise

You conform to others around you, and the values of others influence your own. The people around you can either elevate your game or bring it down. Observe high performers and you'll notice that they surround themselves with people who help them be great. They hang around optimistic and confident people who design their futures.

You can use the Five People Exercise to help you identify and gather your own gritty group.

Step 1. Consider the five people you spend the most time with. Write down three qualities that stand out to you about each person.

_____

_____

_____

_____

_____

Step 2. Reflect on whether these qualities help you get to where you want to go and whether you need to decide to spend more or less time with each person. Ask if each of these people provides positive or negative momentum. Then, put a positive or negative sign by each name to indicate if you need to spend more or less time with the people on your list.

Step 3. Write down five attributes that you need to embody to reach your goals and dreams. These could be attributes that you already have but need to develop more fully, or attributes you do not currently have. Then, identify the friends, colleagues, or teammates who have those qualities from the list above. Circle their names from your list above.

_____

_____

_____

_____

_____

Step 4. Finally, write down five people who are not on your current list but who could support you in getting to where you want to go. List some of the attributes that each person has and record how each person could help push or support you in staying gritty and reaching your vision. Write down how you plan to reach out to these people. Will you email, call, send a message on social media, or approach them face-to-face?

_____

_____

_____

_____

_____

Remember: you can't be exceptional on your own. You need support and a crew of like-minded superstars who believe in your vision and push you to be the very best version of yourself. (p. 219)

CONCLUDING THOUGHTS

Your High Performance Toolbox is getting very full! In High Performers Choose Empowering Emotions, you did the following:

- You outlined the empowering emotions you want to feel more consistently.

- You considered how your past performances can help you be confident.

- You identified a happiness-improving question to recognize and appreciate what you have.

- You considered two ways you can improve your gratitude.

- And you outlined a highlight reel you can use to powerfully practice imagery daily.

Now, take a moment to record the following on your Grit Board:

- 3 empowering emotions that you consistently want to feel.

- 1 happiness-improving question you identified.

- A key phrase from this section such as "Imagine Greatness," "Choose Confidence" or "Choose Happiness!"

My High Performance Power Phrase

I choose positivity. I choose to bring positive energy each day and in each situation. I choose empowering emotions.

8

Own Who You Are

The world's best
make the conscious choice to show up
as themselves every day and in every
interaction. They know who they are
and own who they are.

We can practice authenticity:

we can choose to make a decision to be us and be real instead of trying to be someone we are not.

Own Who You Are

"When writing the story of your life, don't let someone else hold the pen."
—*Anonymous*

Authenticity is a foundation of performance. To be successful in sports, business, and life, you must be yourself. When you are real, people connect with you. People can tell when you are a phony!

"Doing you" can be the bravest battle you fight. But when you "do you," you show your true gifts to the world. You make the choice to let your true self be seen. You are able to reach a whole new level of performance when you are not worried what others think about you. You are not evaluating your worthiness by critics' opinions. Comparison makes us feel like we are never enough: not good enough, smart enough, powerful enough, thin enough, successful enough. The list goes on and on. Comparison is a trap. It can spin us into a tail-chasing frenzy of self-doubt; it's about being "better" than others, not about getting better yourself. The less attention you pay to others around you, the happier and more capable you will become.

When you own your story, you begin to connect with it in a deeper way. You are proud of what you have overcome and who you are now. When you own your story, you give yourself even more control over its next chapter.

Remember that being yourself is how you connect with others. When you are yourself without judgment, you are free to perform to your potential.

Exercise 1: Do You

I'm a big fan of Brene' Brown's work on authenticity. In her book *The Gifts of Imperfection*, she says that authenticity is a practice: it's not something we have or don't have, but a conscious choice of how we want to live. Brown's research suggests that there are some people who consciously practice authenticity daily. The rest of us are authentic some days and not other days. When we mindfully and purposefully practice authenticity, we invite happiness, gratitude, and joy into our lives, and this impacts our performance. As Brown said, we let go of who we think we should be, and embrace who we really are—even though we are not perfect. To "Do You" more often, consider your answers to the following questions.

Step 1. What are a few times that I wasn't "doing me?" What were the consequences? Are there any commonalities in those experiences?

_____

_____

_____

_____

_____

_____

Step 2. What does it mean to "Do Me"?

_____

_____

_____

_____

_____

_____

_____

_____

Step 3. What can I do to "Do Me" more often?

_____

_____

_____

_____

_____

_____

_____

The world needs you and your gifts. Don't hold back!

Exercise 2: Let Go of Comparison

It's easy to get caught up in the competition, to take your eyes off the lane in front of you. It's easy to compare yourself or your performance to others instead of staying focused on your own improvement. We compare our appearance, our businesses, our number of friends, our athletic abilities, our families, our Facebook or Twitter followers, and our belongings to other people's. Comparison makes us feel like we are never enough: not good enough, smart enough, powerful enough, thin enough, athletic enough, successful enough, strong enough, certain enough, extraordinary enough, fast enough. The list goes on and on. Comparison is a trap. It's a thief of joy and can spin us into a tail-chasing frenzy of self-doubt.

Step 1. How have you shifted your eyes toward your competitors' or others' achievements or things? How has this impacted your performance or happiness? What would you like to do instead of comparing yourself to others?

_____

_____

_____

_____

_____

_____

_____

_____

Step 2: Fill in the blank:

I believe I am not _____ enough

when I compare myself to _____.

Step 3: The first choice you can make is to celebrate your progress instead of comparing yourself to that other person. Choose a date either 1, 3, or 5 years ago. Now, in the space below consider the progress you have made toward your goals and dreams since that date.

_____

_____

_____

_____

_____

_____

_____

_____

_____

Focus your energy on being the best you.

Exercise 3: Own Your Story

Your story creates your reality, and your destiny follows the reality you create. When you own your story, you begin to connect with it in a deeper way. You are proud of what you have overcome and who you are now. When we own our story, we take control of our perspective, how we see ourselves, and how we view the world. We might feel ashamed or guilty about our story, which leaves us feeling powerless. But when we own our story, we release the guilt and negativity. We experience empowerment. We can decide to write a brave new ending.

I challenge you to think about your story and create a brave new ending. Here are a few questions to consider:

Step 1. What stories in my life are working? Which are not working?

_____

_____

_____

_____

_____

_____

_____

Step 2. Which story could use a fresh perspective?

_____

_____

_____

_____

_____

_____

_____

Step 3. Which parts of my story are lies and not the complete truth?

_____

_____

_____

_____

_____

_____

Step 4. Which "story" will not allow me to get where I want to be in my life?

_____

_____

_____

_____

_____

_____

_____

_____

Step 5. What's the brave new ending that I want to write for my story?

_____

_____

_____

_____

_____

_____

When you change your story, you change your life.

Exercise 4: Defeat Your Limiting Beliefs

Limiting beliefs are beliefs that constrain us in some way. They can be about others, the world, and ourselves. They are typically broad statements that exist only in our head. We have a lot of limiting beliefs that we may not even be aware of, and these limiting beliefs reflect self-doubt and feelings of unworthiness. Underlying every limiting belief is the idea that we are not good enough. We must address our limiting beliefs because they are what limits us. You have the power right now in the present moment to change your limiting beliefs. Here are the 5 steps to change your limiting beliefs:

Step 1. Identify two limiting beliefs that hold you back from the future you envision. To do this, complete the following prompt:

1. *I believe I cannot expand to my greater potential because:*

_____

_____

_____

_____

2. *I believe I cannot expand to my greater potential because:*

_____

_____

_____

_____

Step 2. Ask yourself, "Do I want to keep holding on to these limiting beliefs?" Consider what you're missing out on by holding onto them. Are you playing small? Are you holding yourself back? Reflect on what you are missing out on if you continue to believe those limiting beliefs.

_____

_____

_____

_____

_____

_____

Step 3. Decide to conquer your limiting beliefs. Say out loud or in your head, "I no longer believe this to be true."

Step 4. Without judgment, replace these two beliefs. Ask yourself which two beliefs would allow you to become all you could be. Write those two beliefs below.

1. _____

_____

_____

2. _____

_____

_____

Step 5. Lastly, prove your new empowering beliefs true. Write below the ways you know your new belief is true. As you move forward with your new beliefs, continue to notice all the ways they are proven true in your life.

1. _____

_____

_____

2. _____

_____

_____

You begin to fly when you address your limiting beliefs. You can move your vision for your future to new heights.

Practice 8
CONCLUDING THOUGHTS

Seriously, you are amazing! With each chapter you are getting mentally strong and gaining more useful strategies for your daily life. In Own Who You Are, you did the following:

- You identified what it means to "do you" and how you can be yourself more often.

- You decided to work to be the best version of yourself and reflected on when you engage in comparison.

- You outlined a brave new ending to your story.

- And you identified two new empowering beliefs you will prove right.

Now, take a moment to record the following on your Grit Board:

- 3 words that describe you when you're "doing you."

- A new empowering belief that you will begin to live by.

- A key phrase from this section such as "Do You," "Be the Best Version of Myself," or "Own My Story!"

My High Performance Power Phrase

The world needs me and my gifts. I will show up as myself and let me true self be seen. I will "do me."

9

Live and Let Go

The world's best
know that people are not perfect.
They are kind to themselves, let go of
their mistakes quickly after learning from
them, and decide to live life full-out.

Self-compassion

is a powerful antidote
to the perfectionist thinking,
stress, and anxiety that
can lead to poor
performance. If we
practice self-compassion,
we are better able
to forgive others, too.

Practice 9

Live and Let Go

"I have not failed. I've just found 10,000 ways that won't work."
—Thomas Edison

The world's best have very high standards. They expect success. Along with high standards can come a difficulty letting go of mistakes. I've found that many elite athletes, talented coaches, and successful entrepreneurs have a hard time with self-compassion, or the practice of being kind to yourself. When I teach them about self-compassion, however, they play and perform more consistently even though they have already reached a high level of success.

All humans are imperfect and mortal. Who ever said you needed to be perfect anyway? Likely no one! But we have this expectation in our mind that we need to be perfect. Showing self-compassion means that you honor that you are human and accept that you are not perfect. When we don't practice self-compassion, we experience frustration, stress, suffering, and self-criticism. Staying gritty and reaching high performance requires adopting the mindset of constant and never-ending improvement. To reach your goals and to stay current and relevant, you need to constantly evolve your skills and mindset. Don't get immersed in your mistakes—self-pity gets you further from where you need to go. Instead, accept that there's always room for improvement and work to be the best you can be.

The practice of self-compassion is giving the same kindness to ourselves that we would give to others. It is about accepting yourself and recognizing you are not perfect.

Exercise 1: Increase Your Self-Compassion by Taking the Best-Friend Challenge

A key in developing and practicing self-compassion is talking to yourself like you would talk to your best friend or family member. Take the Best Friend Challenge and each day this week make a commitment to be kind to yourself. Notice the tone of your self-talk and what you say to yourself. Make an effort to soften your self-critical voice and do so with compassion. You are always listening to yourself, so speak nicely!

To gain self-awareness of the difference between how you talk to yourself compared to how you talk to your best friend, complete the following exercise adopted from pioneering researcher Dr. Kristin Neff:

Step 1. Think about a time or times when your close friend was struggling. How did you respond to your best friend? Reflect on how you would typically respond and what you might say.

_____

_____

_____

_____

Step 2. Now, think about times you are struggling or upset. How do you typically respond to yourself? Reflect on how you would typically respond and what you might say to yourself when you are struggling.

_____

_____

_____

_____

_____

Step 3. What is the difference between how you respond to your best friend and how you respond to yourself? What impacts how you respond differently to a friend? What fears or limiting beliefs impact your response?

_____

_____

_____

_____

Step 4. Write about how you want to respond to yourself in the future. How might things change for you when you decide to respond more compassionately to yourself?

_____

_____

_____

_____

Self-compassion is a habit we form by practicing kindness in the moment many times throughout our day.

Exercise 2: Talk to Your Judge

Judgment is universal. It is a common ailment we all experience. We all judge ourselves and experience the judgment of others, and it can be detrimental to our teams, our families, and ourselves. Judgment compels us to constantly find faults in and around us. When we judge, we see things as bad rather than seeing them as a gift or opportunity. We focus on what is wrong with the situation instead of what is right. We don't see our worthiness and the worthiness of others when we judge.

Address your judge by using the CAR Shift:

Catch it. *Being aware that we all have a judge gives us permission to pay attention and helps us recognize that we are not suffering alone. When you notice and acknowledge your judge, you reduce the judge's power! Identify a time you tend to judge yourself below:*

_____

_____

_____

_____

_____

_____

Address it. *Look for ways to address your judge. Tell your judge why it is not accurate. Start seeing the situation without your judge and ask yourself, "What is real here?" Describe that below.*

_____

_____

_____

_____

_____

_____

_____

Refocus it. _Instead of listening to your judge, get focused on the next step to reach your goals. Move on. Focus your attention elsewhere and decide to be kinder to yourself in the future. Below, identify the next step toward goals you will focus on._

_____

_____

_____

_____

_____

_____

_____

Less judgment and more self-compassion make us feel alive. The world's best work to reduce their judge.

Exercise 3: Adopting a Growth Mindset

According to over thirty years of research by Carol Dweck, a professor at Stanford University, we face challenges with either a "growth mindset" or a "fixed mindset." When we adopt a fixed mindset, we see our ability, intelligence, and athletic talent as fixed at birth and unable to be changed. When we adopt a growth mindset, we believe we can grow and change for the better. We see challenges as exciting and find optimistic ways of explaining adversity. We continuously seek help from others because that is the way we learn and improve. We believe our qualities can improve with effort and constant learning.

One key to developing an optimistic, growth mindset is to catch yourself when you surrender to the pessimistic, fixed mindset. In the boxes below, practice changing a fixed-mindset phrase to a growth-mindset phrase in the first three boxes.

Then, in the remaining boxes, write a fixed-mindset phrase you think or believe. In the box next to it, change that statement to an optimistic growth mindset you want to adopt.

Fixed-Mindset Phrase	*Growth-Mindset Phrase*
"This is just too hard."	
"My boss/coach is so rude to me. He/she doesn't like me."	
"I'll never be able to do that."	

Our set point may be to adopt the pessimistic fixed mindset, to judge the ability of ourselves and others. The key is to catch ourselves when we adopt the fixed mindset.

Exercise 4: Learn, Burn, Return After Mistakes

Failure is inevitable and essential for us to perform at our very best. We often think of failure as any time we don't meet our own expectations or reach our goals. But failure doesn't need to paralyze you. The world's best recognize that failures will occur, and the real enemy is *fear* of failure. The world's best have failed many times, and they view mistakes as mis-takes. They also have an effective way to deal with mistakes, something I call "Learn, Burn, and Return," a catchy strategy for their High Performance Toolbox.

To help you effectively deal with mistakes, apply the Learn, Burn, and Return strategy. Outline a mistake you made in the past so you can know how to apply the strategy in the future. Remember, you can use the strategy any time you are having difficulty letting go of a mistake or failure.

Step 1: Identify a time in the past where you made a mistake that you had difficulty moving on from:

_____

_____

_____

_____

_____

_____

_____

Step 2: **_Learn:_** Consider what you learned from the mistake objectively. While doing so, stay unemotional and focused on what you plan to do in the future instead of on the past. To do this, start a sentence with, "Next time I will

. . ." Think of what you learned in an objective, factual way instead of a subjective, biased way, and avoid taking the mistake to heart. Outline what you will do next time given the mistake you outlined above:

Next time I will . . .

_____

_____

_____

_____

_____

_____

Step 3: **_Burn_**: The next step after learning from the mistake is to burn it. By this I mean let it go. You could use a Burn Phrase such as "Let it go!" "Flush it." "Move on." "Burn it." Or you could use a Burn Action which symbolizes letting your mistake go, such as brushing down your arm with your hand as if you were brushing off the mistake, picking up a piece of grass and letting the mistake go when the blade of grass leaves your hand, or adjusting your headband or your socks to symbolize to yourself that you let the mistake go and are moving on. Identify the Burn Phrase or Action you want to use in the future below:

_____

_____

_____

_____

_____

_____

_____

Step 4: **Return:** After you have learned and burned, it's important to keep your self-talk and body language confident. You must "return" to thinking and feeling confident despite the mistake. Outline how you want your body language to look after a mistake, and the thoughts you want to go through your head as you "return" after the mistake.

_____

_____

_____

_____

_____

**The mindset that you can fail forward will help you relax, get in
the flow zone, and improve your current performance.**

Practice 9
CONCLUDING THOUGHTS

Almost at the finish line! In Live and Let Go, you did the following:

- You increased your self-compassion by taking the best-friend challenge.

- You outlined the CAR shift to reduce your internal judge.

- You learned how you can adopt a growth mindset where you see challenges as exciting.

- And you outlined how you can apply the "Learn, Burn, and Return" strategy the next time you fail or make a mistake.

Now, take a moment to record the following on your Grit Board:

- A Growth Mindset Phrase to keep you focused on improvement.

- A key phrase from this section such as "Be Kind to Myself," "Use the CAR Shift," or "Learn, Burn, Return!"

My High Performance Power Phrase

I am kind to myself. I am doing the best I can. I got it next time!

10

Choose Your Courage Zone

The world's best
feel uncomfortable regularly. When we stay
in our comfort zone, we don't grow.
High performers know that magic happens
in their courage zone.

Yes, you will feel

uncomfortable and experience failure, mistakes, and change in your Courage Zone. But it is the only place where you can reach your full potential or high performance.

Choose Your Courage Zone

"Everything you want is on the other side of fear." —Jack Canfield

When we stay in our comfort zone, we do not grow. We just survive, settle for less, and are okay with being like everyone else. We let fear, doubt, regret, and insecurity get the best of us, resulting in mediocrity.

Growth happens outside of your comfort zone. You try new things, connect with new people, talk in front of large groups, and conquer your fears. You act with courage and bravery. You take calculated risks, turning "impossible" into "I'm possible," and pursue your dreams.

This Courage Zone is the place where you'll build up grit. It is the only place where true happiness occurs, because happiness doesn't happen when you wonder what you could have been; it happens when you are growing. When you push past perceived barriers and limitations, you'll get comfortable being uncomfortable, always striving for the next step in your improvement.

A moment is all it takes! Courage is not the absence of fear or doubt, but it *is* the ability to do something that is scary. We can train our minds to act more courageously every day. See your step into your Courage Zone as adventurous and exciting, not scary or nerve-racking.

Take the leap and accept the 7-Day Challenge. Commit to doing one thing that is uncomfortable or a little scary each day this week.

Exercise 1: Identify My Courage Zone

Few people live daily in their Courage Zone. Instead, they settle in their comfort zone, playing small with their life; doing the things everyone else does; just surviving rather than standing out; and letting doubt, insecurity, and fear eat at them. But high performers think differently. You, my friend, are a high performer! High performers choose Courage Zone activities where they play big with their life, act with courage and bravery every day, do things that they are afraid of, choose hard or difficult things, and live a life of no regrets pursuing self-discovery and their big dreams.

COMFORT ZONE

Safety and Security, Playing Small, Settling, Things I Usually Do, Just Surviving, Don't Stand Out, Doubt, Insecurity, Mediocrity, Fear, Depression

Most People Live Here.

COURAGE ZONE
Where Magic Occurs

Courage and Bravery, Playing Big, Things I've Never Tried, Things I am Afraid Of, Opportunity, Hard and Difficult, Okay Standing Out, Risk, No Regrets, Self-Discovery, Financial Freedom, Potential, Your Authentic Self, Fulfillment, Pursing your Dreams, High Performance

Few People Live Here.

Choosing your Courage Zone is a daily choice. Identify in the circles the following:

- 2-3 Comfort Zone activities that you know you need to give up today

- 2-3 Courage Zone activities that you commit to engaging in today

It is true that your Courage Zone activities are always changing. In one year, the activities you listed in your Courage Zone will likely be different if you are pushing yourself this year. Therefore, repeat this exercise often to keep embracing your Courage Zone daily!

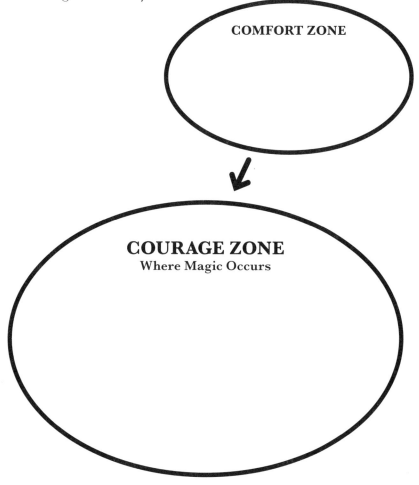

When I encounter something that makes me uncomfortable this week, I'll go for it. I'll remind myself to choose courage and make it happen.

Exercise 2: My Biggest Fears

To bring awareness to your fear, make a list of things that you fear or are afraid to do. Start each statement beginning with *"If I weren't afraid, I would . . ."* For example, a list like this might include statements such as: "If I weren't afraid, I would compete in an Ironman, go after the starting spot on the team, or submit my resume for a new job."

Then, turn these fears into "I know" statements. Your list might become, "I know I can compete in an Ironman, I know I can earn the starting spot on the team, and I know I can submit my resume for a new job." Post your new list of "I knows" where you can see it daily to remind yourself of what you know.

"If I weren't afraid, I would . . .	*"I know . . .*
"If I weren't afraid, I would . . .	*"I know . . .*
"If I weren't afraid, I would . . .	*"I know . . .*
"If I weren't afraid, I would . . .	*"I know . . .*

This week when I feel fear, I'll remember that everyone experiences fear when they are growing and learning. It simply means that I am doing something important and meaningful.

Exercise 3: Turn Impossible = I'm Possible

Impossible is brief. Impossible is short-lived. Impossible is not permanent. As Muhammad Ali said, "Impossible is not a fact. It is an opinion. It is not a declaration. It is a dare!" The world's best view the impossible as a challenge or dare. When people say, "That's impossible!" they say, "Watch me do it!" They do not put limits on their abilities or achievements. They defy limits. They move boundaries. They push past other people's restrictions. They consider all of the ways they can make it happen.

Step 1. Consider what you think is impossible for you to accomplish. Then, write these impossibles into "What if . . ." questions. For example, perhaps you think it is impossible for you to get into the best shape of your life, make a million dollars, or run an ultramarathon. Put those things into questions like, "What if I got in the best shape of my life?" and "What if I made a million dollars?" and "What if I ran an ultramarathon?" Continue until you have at least ten questions.

"What if . . .

_____

_____ *"*

"What if . . .

_____

_____ *"*

"What if . . .

_____

_____ *"*

"What if . . .

_____

_____ *"*

"What if . . .

_____

_____ *"*

"What if . . .

_____

_____ *"*

"What if . . .

_____

_____ *"*

"What if . . .

_____

_____ *"*

"What if . . .

_____

_____ *"*

Step 2. Consider what you have already accomplished that you once thought was impossible. My guess is that you have done the impossible many times in your life! Make a list of at least five of your impossibles; read it when you feel tempted to give up or listen to your critics!

I once thought it was impossible to:

_____

_____

I once thought it was impossible to:

_____

_____

I once thought it was impossible to:

_____

_____

I once thought it was impossible to:

_____

_____

I once thought it was impossible to:

_____

_____

Step 3. What impossible feat, goal, or dream do you need to reconnect to today? Write it below!

_____

_____

_____

_____

_____

_____

_____

People rarely outperform their goals or dreams. They rarely achieve more then they set out to. Today, reconnect with your impossible!

Exercise 4: Go for the Gold!

When it comes to commitment, 99 percent is hard, 100 percent is easy. Let me explain.

When you are 100 percent committed, you don't let excuses get in the way. The 100 percent commitment keeps you focused. It frees up energy so you don't have to decide in the moment. Your decision is already made, no matter what. You give it your all. You reduce the excuses and keep them out of your mind. You don't play mind games, and you don't go halfway. You are all in.

Let's get clear on your commitment with the 100 Percent Committed Exercise:

Step 1. Write down the "gold medal" you want to be 100 percent committed to. What is worthy of your 100 percent commitment? What deserves your time and attention? Pick one thing and make a commitment by writing it down. It's now a nonnegotiable.

_____

_____

_____

_____

_____

_____

_____

_____

Step 2. Make a list of the key habits and daily disciplines necessary to ensure you are 100 percent committed to your "gold medal." What must you adhere to every day? Perhaps it's 100 sit-ups every day, running five miles, calling two new potential clients, mediating each morning, shooting 200 free throws each day, or reading for an hour every day.

_____

_____

_____

_____

_____

_____

_____

_____

_____

_____

_____

_____

Step 3. Write down what you need to start, stop, and continue to do to reach the 100 percent commitment.

START: What are the habits you need to start to be 100 percent all-in?

_____

_____

_____

_____

STOP: What do you need to stop so you avoid the 99 percent commitment?

_____

_____

_____

_____

CONTINUE: What do you need to continue so you are 100 percent all-in?

_____

_____

_____

_____

If you are 100 percent committed to something, you will do it regardless of how you feel.

CONCLUDING THOUGHTS

Here you are: at the end of this book, with 10 new habits and 52 new strategies to support them. Here in Choose Your Courage Zone, you did the following:

- You outlined the activities in your Courage Zone and Comfort Zones and committed to the 7-Day Challenge.

- You recorded your biggest fears and changed them to "I know . . ." statements.

- You changed your "impossibles" to "I'm possible" and reminded yourself you have already done several "impossibles."

- And you finalized your commitment to your "gold medal" goal by being 100 percent committed and outlining the daily discipline needed to get there.

Now, take a moment to record the following on your Grit Board:

- Your new list of "I know . . ." statements.

- Your "gold medal" you are 100 percent committed to.

- A key phrase from this section such as "Choose My Courage Zone," "Impossible = I'm Possible!" or "Go for the Gold!"

My High Performance Power Phrase:

I choose my Courage Zone over my Comfort Zone. I will play big, try new things, and act with courage and bravery. I get comfortable being uncomfortable.

Free Resources to Go Beyond Grit

This workbook provides strategies and tools to help you develop a High Performance Mindset to reach new levels of your potential. To help you apply the information provided, I've created bonuses for you at beyondgrit.com/bonus.

If you want to get an automatic email when my next book is released, you can sign up at www.cindrakamphoff.com. Your email address will never be shared and you can unsubscribe at any time.

Word-of-mouth is crucial for any author's success. If you enjoyed the book, please consider leaving an online review, even if it's just a line or two. Your review would make all the difference in the world! I am grateful for you!

Finally, I am here to help. If you'd like me to come speak, work with your team/group, or work with you individually, you can reach me at (507) 327-9193 or cindra@cindrakamphoff.com. Please share your ideas, feedback, and questions by emailing me or finding me on Twitter @Mentally_Strong. Add #beyondgrit to your tweet or share a picture of your Grit Board.

The next level is calling you. Stay gritty and mentally strong, my friend!

Book's website: beyondgrit.com
Author's website: cindrakamphoff.com
Twitter: @Mentally_Strong
Facebook: facebook.com/drcindrakamphoff
Instagram: instagram.com/cindrakamphoff/
Email: cindra@cindrakamphoff.com
Podcast: cindrakamphoff.com/podcast